DADAsS

**VOTED #1
SURVIVAL GUIDE
FOR SH**SCARED
NEWBIE DADS**

OLIVER KULT

FOREWORD BY CHE DURENA

Book Cover Graphic Design by Sebastien Stewart

Illustration by Andy Bélanger

ISBN: 9798218397616

FOREWORD BY CHE DURENA

You want to be a dad? Unless you're gonna leverage this crotch goblin's cuteness into smashing single moms you might want to reconsider.

It's hard to stay up until 3am playing vids with the boys when your days are spent with some freeloader sucking up all your time, money and energy. Seriously, the only thing your spawn is gonna deteriorate more then your ability to have fun is your sleep cycle, and for what? Love?!

That's not love, it's a chore. 6am Coke binges and unprotected sex, that's love.

Watching your jizz grow from diarrhea factory to cog in the machine is pretty mediocre, it's probably gonna work at Arby's. Save all the effort from catering to selfish mini-me and spend it on yourself, learn the piano, go to Japan, try molly at an end concert while you're in Japan. You have so much life to live and you're gonna throw it away for a twenty-something year investment that could be mid! Give your head a shake.

If you decide to disregard my warning and conceive a self center money pit with a 40% chance of developing ADHD, craft a second identity you keep secret from your family. If things get rocky use that alter ego to bail on those losers.

Now enjoy this book, it'll be the only survival guide you need, and follow me you fucking idiots. @ chedurena

AUTHOR'S NOTE

This book, *Dadass*, is dedicated to the three VIPs in my crazy circus of a dad's life. First up, the queen of my heart and the tolerator of my insanity, my smoking hot wife, Victoria. Babe, not only did you not run for the hills when I said, "Hey, I'm gonna write a book," but you also didn't lock me in a padded room when I scribbled notes at 3 a.m. because "inspiration struck." You gave me the freedom to chase this wild dream, even when it meant I'd occasionally vanish away from playtime at the beach, mumbling about chapters and plot twists. For that, I owe you big-time. Honestly, without you, *Dadass* would just be a crazy idea I shouted about over beers to my close friends and probably end up being something I'd regret not doing on my deathbed. You're the rockstar behind this wannabe writer. *Dadass* is as much yours as it is mine, and if this thing wins any awards, I'm putting your name on the trophy too. Love you more than emo kids love eyeliner.

And then there's you two, Landon & Skyler, the epic duo who turns every day into an insane adventure—or a test of patience, depending on how many walls you've decided to turn into your personal art gallery with my fucking pens. Boys, by the time you're reading this, this old book of dad wisdom and shenanigans will probably be buried under a decade of new memes and whatever futuristic entertainment you're into. Maybe books are vintage cool now, like vinyls or sanity. I hope so.

Landon, my man, as I'm hammering out these words on the laptop, you're seven years old—or "seven and a half," as you insist with all the seriousness of a politician. You're currently sitting a few inches from me, watching *Matilda* for the eighth time this year. And let me tell you, the "bruh" phase? Not a fan. Every time you drop a "bruh" instead of "dad," a part of me dies inside. I miss the "daddy" days, but hey, time marches on, and apparently so does vocabulary.

I don't know why you think I like being called "Bruh" but I don't, so stop it.

By now, though, you're probably navigating the stormy seas of teenage angst, and we've likely had our rounds in the ring (metaphorically, I hope). You might even think your old man's just some fossil with outdated references and embarrassing dad jokes. But deep down, I hope we've racked up enough wild stories together told around summer vacation campfires that you're secretly thinking, *Damn, Daddy's got some "cool" under those gray hairs.* If not, well, buckle up and dive into this book, "bruh." Your dad's cooler and a lot wilder than you think.

Now, Skyler. Ah, Skyler, my very own whirlwind of chaos, the family's resident surfer dude with golden locks that would make Jason Momoa weep with envy. Yeah, Mommy might call you her "Aquaman," but let's be honest: You're more like a Tasmanian devil, or "SkySky" when we're feeling extra familial and loverboy. The reason I had the balls to put pen to paper (or fingers to keyboard) and dive into the madness that is fatherhood is all thanks to you, kiddo. You've been flipping my world upside down and challenging every preconceived notion I had about being a dad since you decided to grace us with your presence.

Let's get something straight, though: I hope to all that is holy and slightly unholy that you don't crack open this book until you're at least sixteen. Why? The profanity. The words in this book are like if a sailor and a truck driver had a baby, and that baby wrote a book. But knowing your rebellious streak, you're probably sneaking peeks at the book at fourteen, towering over me and bench-pressing more than I could on my best day.

But just know this: Deciding to expand the family was one thing. Actually making it happen? That's where the plot thickens, and not just in a "let's get busy and hope for the best" kind of way. Because believe me, dude, we tried a lot. No, sir. We're talking full-on, sci-fi-level ni-vitro fertilization. The journey to bring you into this world was more intense than any action movie—it was like a mission to Mars, but instead of a spaceship, we had doctors, and instead of astronauts, we had...well, sperm in cups and eggs.

The essence of *Dadass*—this whole crazy ride of a book—is rooted in my lifelong dream to be a dad. And you, Skyler, are the living, breathing (and constantly moving) proof that dreams do come true, albeit with a little scientific nudge. Going through the in-vitro process to have you wasn't just about adding another player to the Kult team; it was about completing our family, about turning that dream into a fucking reality.

My life, our lives, wouldn't be the same without you.

Love you all three...this book is for y'all.

PREFACE

To label this pile of pages an "autobiography" would be as pretentious as a peacock in a top hat (or Mister Peanut, little pretentious bastard), and let's face it, it'd just be me stroking my own ego. I'm no hotshot celebrity, nor am I deluded enough to think my life's a roller coaster you'd want to strap into for hours or days if you're a slow reader.

Did I tie the knot with a hot pornstar? Hell yeah, I did. Star in a reality TV circus? Guilty as charged. Rock out as a reading barber on stages across Russia, France, Canada, and the good ol' USA, making thousands lose their minds and learn shit they'd never thought about? Damn right. Ever found myself handcuffed and thrown in the back seat of a stinky police car by foreign cops? *Sí, señor*, a thrilling international incident. And what about being blasted and coked out of my mind, duking it out in Brooklyn at 2 a.m. with five gang members over a damn McDonald's order? Check and check. Wild, right?

But let me tell you, none of that compares to the real insane ride of my life: fatherhood.

I penned this book not as some wise sage, but as a dad to two ankle-biters who somehow aged me forty years in just seven. I was a green twenty-three when my first kid popped into the world. Ready for fatherhood? Pfft, at that age, we're all just overgrown kids with a license to drink and drive (not at the same time ideally). Hell, isn't there a myth that a guy's dick isn't fully cooked until twenty-four? So, if your manhood's still in the oven, are you really prepped to raise a mini-you? It's a tougher question than you'd think. I've adored being a dad from day one, sure, but I've also been screwing up since then too.

Every time I think I've nailed this badass dad gig, life throws a curveball, and there I am, back to square one, figuring out this fatherhood crap all over again. Having to always introspect and see how I can do better next time. It's hard, like "trying to solve a Rubik's cube while drunk" hard, but damn, it's beautiful.

So here's the deal, this book's for you, the future dad, the newbie dad, or the veteran dad drowning in guilt for not being Mr. Perfect Parent. Spoiler: You'll never hit that mark. But, hopefully, this book gives you a chuckle, makes you feel less alone in the dad-jungle, and eases that guilt a bit.

Fatherhood's tough as fuck, but hang in there. If you've got enough love and enough guts and accept that you're the only one who can morph into the kickass dad your kids need, then you're golden. Enjoy the read, bro .

CHAPTER 1:

THE FATHERHOOD DREAM

I remember that day in fifth grade like it was tattooed on the inside of my eyelids. The teacher, whose name escapes me but whose penchant for sporting braces at an age when most people are fretting over retirement plans, is etched in my brain. Now, these weren't your garden-variety braces; we're talking full metal jacket, the kind that picked up radio signals from distant galaxies. The ones with the stupid elastics holding them together like her jaws were going to split open without it.

And her boobs? Let's just say they were so fucking monumental, they deserved their own zip code. No judgment, though, please—at ten years old, my world revolved around two things: avoiding homework and the mystique of boobs.

The day kicked off with the kind of question that gives existential crises to anxious adults: "What do you want to be when you grow up?" The classroom buzzed with the typical clichés: heroic career dreams. Half the guys wanted to be firefighters, complete with their own Dalmatian sidekick, or cops (gross).

A couple of them aimed for the stars—literally, dreaming of being astronauts. I bet none of them got further than a Star Wars marathon on their couch while indulging a full bag of Cheetos.

Then there were the mini-mes, kids who idolized their dads so much they wanted to photocopy their careers. It was like watching a parade of mini accountants, lawyers, and whatever else paid the bills in suburban households.

As for me, my dream was to hit the ice in the NHL. The only problem? My skating skills were as graceful as a three-legged rhino on roller skates. And my parents' bank account laughed in the face of sports fees. If the sport involved buying more than one item to participate, it was out of the question. So, there I was, telling the class about my "dream" of becoming a mechanic. Not because I had a burning passion for grease and gears, but because it seemed like a solid plan B. Plus, I figured mechanics got to drive cool cars, and in my ten-year-old mind, cool cars equated to an endless supply of street cred and, hopefully, a tattooed girlfriend who wasn't imaginary.

Looking back, I can see my ten-year-old self, wide-eyed and clueless, declaring my fake dream to be a mechanic. It's laughable now. My entire car education was fueled by fantasies of *The Fast and the Furious* and the digital streets of *Need for Speed Underground 2* on Xbox. I mean, who wouldn't want to live in a world where cars practically flew and every street race ended with a bombshell Latina model hanging on your arm? Plus, *Pimp My Ride* had me convinced that every clunker could transform into a nightclub on wheels with enough LCD screens and subwoofers. Who cares about Ferraris when you got a Tercel but Xzbit's got your back, right?

But here's the kicker: I knew jack shit about cars. My old man wasn't exactly a gearhead—the closest he got to a car hobby was cursing at the TV during Formula 1 races the one time he watched it. My car experience was limited to two things: the intoxicating smell of new tires and the dizzying fumes at the gas station. Yeah, we still had those full-service stations back in the day, a lost relic in a world speeding toward self-service and electric bullshit.

I nailed the presentation, though. Got an "A" and everything. But let's face it, that career choice stuck to me as well as water sticks to a greased-up duck. Fast forward to now, and my car knowledge is embarrassingly basic. Stick shift? Might as well be rocket science. Changed a flat tire once, and that was after a YouTube tutorial and a string of expletives that would make a sailor blush.

Oil changes? I'm the golden goose for those mechanics—they see me coming and cha-ching! I'm paying top dollar for what I'm sure is a five-minute job my Mexican mechanic can do with one eye open (which he actually does since he only has one eye after losing one in a fight with a stray dog in his teenage years).

And those warning lights on my dashboard? I've adopted a "don't ask, don't tell" policy. If the car hasn't exploded yet, it's probably fine, right?

My relationship with cars died a sad, unceremonious death somewhere around *Tokyo Drift*. *The Fast and the Furious* franchise lost its cool factor the second they had over thirty minutes without a scene with Vin Diesel, and with it went my boyhood dreams of being the next Toretto. Now, I'm just another schmuck in an SUV, nodding along as the mechanic rattles off terms like "transmission fluid" and "differential." I don't have a damn clue, but I nod like I do, hoping not to get totally fleeced. It's a far cry from the neon-lit, NOS-fueled dreams of my youth, but hey, at least I can parallel park this beast without taking out a mailbox. Small victories, right?

Finding the right career was like trying to find a needle in a haystack, if the haystack was on fire and the needle was actually a bottle of cheap booze. My parents, bless their hearts, started sweating bullets as high school came to a close. They watched with a mix of horror and fascination as the only career I seemed remotely qualified for—gas station pump jockey—went the way of the dodo. Full-service gas stations became as rare as a sober thought at a frat party (not that I know what a frat party is actually, for I've only seen it in movies).

I could almost hear their nightly prayers, begging the universe not to let their precious son become the only guy in town whose career peak was mastering the "regular or premium" query. But let's face it, my teenage years weren't exactly a highlight reel of promising career moves. Most of my time was spent perfecting the art of being spectacularly average at everything for someone who was barely showing up to class. Math? I had the number skills of a drunk monkey. Science? My last experiment involved seeing how many marshmallows I could stuff into my mouth (spoiler: it's a lot).

As the end of high school loomed like a giant, menacing cloud of "what the hell do I do now," my parents' stress levels skyrocketed. Their little angel (lol), who once dreamt of pimping rides and tearing up the NHL, was now dangerously close to having his most marketable skill be his uncanny ability to identify different flavors of Doritos blindfolded.

And let me tell you, the career advice I got was about as useful as a chocolate teapot. Guidance counselors with their cliché lines like, "Follow your dreams" and "You can be anything you want to be." Great, Karen, I'll just be over here dreaming of being a rockstar in the first metalcore band to sign to a major record label.

So, as high school graduation loomed, my career prospects were looking about as bright as a black hole. I was about as prepared for the real world as a penguin is for a desert marathon. But fear not, this isn't a tale of woe and unemployment. It's just the bumpy, somewhat hilarious road of a now successful guy who was about as clueless as a cat in a dog show when it came to figuring out his life.

But hey, life has a funny way of working out. Sometimes you've got to wade through a river of crap to find that golden nugget. Or in my case, stumble blindly into it while trying to figure out how not to be a complete disaster. Stick around—the ride only gets wilder from here.

Isn't it wild, the idea that at the ripe old age of sixteen or seventeen, society expects you to have your whole life mapped out? That's the time when you're supposed to start prepping for college or university, choosing a career path as if you've got all the answers.

While working on this book, I dug up some stats that blew my mind: A study in the USA found that roughly 24 percent of teenagers end up snagging their dream jobs from childhood at some point in their lives. Even more staggering, up to 10 percent cling to that same job for their entire working existence. That's a significant chunk, sure, but it also means a whopping 76 percent of us take a detour somewhere between our sandbox dreams and the stark reality of early adulthood.

Count me in as a proud member of that 76 percent. My career path has zigzagged more than my romantic escapades pre-marriage (and that's saying something).

I still have vivid memories of career day back in high school—a dreary, uninspiring affair that could've been a scene straight out of *The Office*. Remember the "Job Fair" episode with the Dunder Mifflin Paper stand? Exactly like that. Every booth was a parade of soul-sucking 9-5 gigs, each one screaming a lifetime of monotony. It felt like signing up for a lifelong sentence of high school, trapped behind a desk, toiling away at tasks dished out by someone earning an extra ten bucks an hour than you. It's no different from the school grind—sit down, shut up, do what you're told. But even back then, with barely a clue about who I was or what I wanted, I knew one thing for damn sure: I wasn't cut out to be some mindless drone, a cog in the corporate machine.

That's the thing about life—it's not a straight line. It's a mess of scribbles, full of wrong turns and detours. And that's okay. It's better than okay. It's what makes the journey interesting.

So there I was, barely eighteen, convinced I'd stumbled upon my life's calling—and, let's be real, it was pretty badass. I started racking up gigs as a tour manager for metal bands. We're not talking about those big-name headliners like Metallica that fill stadiums; these were the gritty, underground groups with band name logos that are unreadable that could pull in a modest crowd of 100 to 500 diehard fans a night across the USA and Canada. That's pretty damn impressive considering most of their lyrics sound like a bear gargling nails—indecipherable but weirdly captivating.

In my head, at that time, I'd hit the jackpot. I was on the fast track to becoming a rockstar, minus the actual musical talent. I wasn't talented enough to be a lead guitarist or a rhythm one. I had to come to terms with the fact that if I joined a band, it would be as the loser slapping the bass. Picture this: I'm the youngest dude on the tour bus, and by bus, I mean a Ford Econoline that's one pothole away from becoming a spectacular roadside fireworks show. This rust bucket, dragging a trailer held together by hope, duct tape, and prayers to Satan, was my chariot.

Despite being the baby of the group, I was often the one holding the reins. My job? Seemingly simple:

keep track of the promoters; call them a day or two before the show to figure out the logistics like load-in times and where the hell we could park our vehicular time bomb without getting towed. For most of these bands, they were one parking ticket away from bankruptcy. Oh, and I handled the cash. It wasn't like these bands were swimming in money; they were paid in peanuts, literally sometimes, which made my job of managing expenses, payouts, and merch sales kinda like being a glorified piggy bank.

But you know what? It was more responsibility than any kid my age usually had. While my peers were flipping burgers or frosting cupcakes, I was crunching numbers and making sure a bunch of tattooed, leather-clad musicians didn't end up playing in an empty room or sleeping in their van because I'd screwed up. It was a crash course in growing the hell up, and I loved every chaotic, unpredictable minute of it.

Touring with metal bands, man, it was a whole different beast than I'd pictured in my head. Let's set the scene: The year was 2011, not the swingin' '50s, where a dime could buy you a steak dinner. My salary? Just enough to keep my phone buzzing and the car I wasn't driving back home from getting repoed. And since I was still crashing in the luxurious confines of my parents' basement, my financial needs were, shall we say, minimal. If I had enough for weed and energy drinks, I had enough to live.

The per diem was a joke—five to ten bucks a day. You couldn't even bribe a kid with that kind of cash. So, there I was, living off a gourmet diet of cold Chef Boyardee straight from the can, ramen noodles, and the daily energy drink—or should I say, energy drinks. And yeah, before you ask, I did once use an energy drink as broth for my ramen. Desperate times, desperate measures, and all that jazz. Plus, when you're either high or drunk, cold pasta and caffeinated soup seem like Michelin-star meals. Call me the ghetto Gordon Ramsey.

But even I had to admit, something had to give. I needed more cash, and quick. Robbing a bank fleetingly crossed my mind, but let's face it—at 140 pounds and sporting what some ladies I was having one-night stands with might call a "bubble butt," I wasn't exactly cut out for a life of crime, and prison orange is not my color.

Then, like some bizarre twist of fate, everything changed during a day off. The band and I, broke as hell, stayed in a $40-a-night Motel 6, the kind of place where even the cockroaches have given up. We couldn't afford a haircut, not even from Suzy at the mall, who's been dishing out the same tragic bowl cut since Reagan was president. So, what did we do? We turned that dingy motel bathroom into our own makeshift barbershop. It passed the vibe check.

That night, armed with a fresh pair of hair clippers meant for ball shaving that we got at a Flying J gas station, I became an impromptu barber. Blasting Wu-Tang Clan from my ancient iPhone 3, I went full-on gangster barber mode. I didn't have face tattoos at that time, but I was already imagining what I'd look like with a straight blade beside my eye. To my shock, and everyone else's, the haircut didn't suck. It was actually... good. Like, really good.

From that moment, I declared myself the official tour barber. Those clippers became my weapon of choice, my tool of trade. It wasn't just about saving a few bucks anymore; it was about finding a new skill, a new part of me I never knew existed. And let me tell you, nothing boosts your street cred like being able to give a decent haircut in a seedy motel room with a soundtrack of gritty hip-hop and the lingering scent of cheap cologne and desperation. It was a game-changer, and little did I know, it was just the beginning.

From that game-changing night in the Motel 6, I started hustling like a real back-alley entrepreneur. I charged a whopping five bucks a pop for haircuts—and by haircuts, I mean a quick snip-snip in the most glamorous of locales: the handicap stall of various dingy venue bathrooms. Not every haircut was a masterpiece. Hell, most were more "abstract art" than "high fashion," but damn, it was fun, and practice was helping me improve.

The extra cash was sweet—I upgraded from starvation chic to a luxurious two meals a day, plus a bonus snack (usually a bag of candy, because who needs vitamins when you've got sugar?). But the real treasure was the stories. I became this weird confessional booth for road-weary band members, merch guys, and even the occasional fan. They'd spill their guts while I tried not to butcher their hair too badly. I heard tales that were hilarious, terrifying, and sometimes straight-up illegal (the drunker the client, the more illegal the story). But the best stories? They always came from the dads. Something about those heartfelt dad tales, man, they hit different.

Barely two years into this touring circus, a few months into my illustrious career as a makeshift barber, and something inside me started to shift. Free booze, cool musicians, and fucking girls in every city—it was the dream, right? But there it was, creeping up on me like a hangover on a Sunday morning—the urge to settle down. Me, not even twenty, suddenly craving the whole suburban dream: a house with a white picket fence, a wife, kids running across the yard, and yeah, even a cliché golden retriever. What the actual fuck, right? Was I homesick, or just sick of being perpetually hammered? Is that why Mike

Jagger has eight kids? Was adulthood smacking me in the face? Or had all those dad stories turned my brain to mush?

Honestly, it was a bit of everything. For the first time ever, I had something resembling a goal. Sure, I was still clueless about the big picture—was I going to be the world's most badass barber forever? Could I even survive outside my parental safety net? Should I keep my hair short or grow it out and dye it some wild color? Who the hell knew?

I did like every unstable person does in doubt, I got a tattoo. Hoping it would fix my feelings. But it didn't.

Amidst all that uncertainty, one thing was crystal clear: I was going to be a dad someday. Not just any dad, but the coolest, tattoo-covered, storytelling, life-lesson-teaching kind of dad. A dad who could spin yarns about touring with metal bands and cutting hair in the crappiest of bathrooms. A dad who turned a wild, aimless youth into something resembling a decent human being. Yeah, that was the dream—the new dream. A fatherhood dream. And it was weirdly exciting.

Is it fucking insane to be nudging twenty, still a card-carrying member of the Teenage Mutant Ninja Hormones club, yet already itching for the dad life? Maybe it is, maybe I was crazy, but who the hell cares? After traveling all around America, snipping hair and chatting up dudes from every corner of the country as an international musical scene barbering guru, I've heard it from the horse's mouth: Even the most commitment-phobic bros, deep down in places they don't talk about at parties, have this itch to one day be someone's dad. They all secretly yearn for that magical moment when a tiny human looks up at them and says, "My daddy's the best," and actually means it. Just writing it makes me smile.

I stumbled upon this piece in *USA Today*, and it blew my fucking mind. A study they mentioned stated that eight out of ten guys harbor dreams of fatherhood. That's 80 percent, man. In a room full of ten dudes, you can't even get eight to agree on what booze to buy, let alone anything significant. And yet, here we are, almost unanimously voting for diaper duty. It's wild, right? But if that's the case, why the hell are there so many deadbeat dads out there? If the majority of us are supposedly wired for fatherhood, where's the disconnect?

This led me down a rabbit hole of thoughts. I might be hella wrong here but is it because we've never been schooled on what it means to be a badass dad? Or maybe it's just our naivety, thinking we can handle the hurricane of responsibility that comes with raising a mini-me. It's probably a mix of both. After all, how can you ace a test you never studied for? I couldn't in high school. How could I do it as an adult?

So there I was, this almost-twenty-year-old barber-slash-philosopher, wrestling with these existential dad dilemmas. Would I cut it as a dad? What's the secret sauce to dad greatness? Is it just one of those pie-in-the-sky dreams that only happens for the chosen few?

It's funny, in a way. Here I am, a guy who's made a living out of turning crappy haircuts into passable ones in the back of a van or a dingy motel bathroom, now pondering the mysteries of fatherhood. It's like I've gone from cutting hair to cutting through the fabric of life's great mysteries. Fuck, man, do I sound smart writing this. But hey, if there's one thing I've learned, it's that sometimes the most profound revelations come to you in the most unexpected places—like while you're trimming some dude's mullet in a Motel 6 bathroom.

Dreaming of being a dad is a whole other ballgame compared to those who drool over Lamborghinis or get their kicks scaling Everest. You can be a total numbnut and still zip around in a luxury car (seriously, have you seen how some of these BMW drivers operate?), or be a few fries short of a Happy Meal and climb a big-ass snowy rock. But at the tender age of twenty, I had this crazy idea in my head that to be a rad dad, I had to morph into this ultimate adult—the kind you see in those cheesy family movies where the dad's chilling in a Central Park mansion, somehow affording to spend all day playing with his adopted mouse son. What the actual fuck, right?

Then fatherhood hit me like a ton of bricks. Twice, for good measure. All those neat little constructs I had? They exploded into a billion pieces the moment my first kid burst onto the scene. Here's a newsflash for ya: whatever life you've built for yourself, it's going to get flipped upside down the second a tiny, screaming poop-machine enters your world. I was clueless. Sure, I'd skimmed through the parenting books (reading in diagonal) how to change diapers, what not to feed the ankle-biters, and the all-important rule: don't shake the baby. But those books don't prep you for the real deal.

Writing this book now, it's like killing two birds with one stone. I'm here to tell you, if I can go from being a booze-swigging, drug-dabbling mess to a father of two, you've got this in the bag (most of the time). I'm hoping that sharing my messed-up journey from party animal to papa bear will not only give you a sense of reassurance and maybe a couple of laughs, but also serve as a bit of a pat on the back for me. It's a reminder of how far I've come since that first flicker of the fatherhood dream lit up in my brain and tugged at my heartstrings.

Your dream of being a badass dad? It's not just a pipe dream. It's totally doable. Trust in that. This path you're on, stumbling toward fatherhood, is the most hardcore, life-altering, mind-blowing journey you'll ever embark on. And let me tell you, it's worth every sleepless night, every diaper disaster, and every moment of self-doubt. You're in for the ride of your life, and it's going to be epic.

CHAPTER 2:

IS SHE THE ONE?

My first girlfriend was a Vietnamese girl, daughter of the only Vietnamese restaurant owners in my sleepy, agriculture-obsessed, French-speaking hometown. A town where the scent of fresh manure was as casual as having parents who are cousins. And yet, their restaurant was surprisingly a hit among the French rednecks. I mean, who can resist a steaming bowl of Pho, right? I know I couldn't, especially when it came with a side of the owner's daughter—long, dark hair, eyes you could get lost in, and a smile that could light up the darkest of rooms (and thank God, she was one of the few girls around without a mouthful of metal or a whole field of strawberries in the face).

I was about fourteen when we dated, light-years away from any fatherhood fantasies. But let's be real, any guy who's tiptoed into puberty and started having those awkward, yet pleasing, wet dreams has wondered, at least once, what a mini-me with his high school crush would look like. It's fucking nuts, right? There I was, a hormonal time bomb, fantasizing about future kids with a girl I hadn't even rounded first base with (at that point, my most intimate experiences were with my hand and a few sacrificial socks).

Let's take a quick detour into Biology 101. We, as men, are practically hardwired for procreation. It's all about primal instincts, baby. Sure, women are the miraculous life-creators, the womb wizards. But let's not forget, it takes two to tango, and it starts with a pair of fully loaded cojones. Back in the caveman days, guys had to duke it out, alpha-male style, for the right to spread their seed. The goal? Knock up as many cave-ladies as possible, ensuring the survival of their hairy, club-wielding lineage. Don't believe me? Google it. I'm no historian teacher (even though I'd clearly give entertaining classes) but I've done my fucking research for this book.

Fast forward to the modern day, and thankfully, we've traded in UFC-style mating rituals for something slightly more civilized (but arguably just as brutal)—the ever-looming, anxiety-inducing relationship gauntlet. No longer do we duke it out in the ring for the right to procreate with the most fertile woman. Now, we're navigating the minefield of family BBQs, friend interrogations, and those awkward water cooler conversations with coworkers who are way too invested in our love lives. Cut me some slack, Nancy, I don't even fucking like you.

"Is she the one?" they ask, with that look in their eyes that's a weird mix of hope, skepticism, and a touch of voyeurism. How the hell are you supposed to answer that? Sure, she might check all the boxes: she's got a heart of gold (the most important), she whips up a mean lasagna that almost gives Nonna a run for her money (not really but you have to tell her that), she's got your back like a badass sidekick, and let's not forget—she turns the bedroom into a scene straight out of a porn set.

But does that mean she's the one you want in your corner when it's 2 a.m., you're knee-deep in shitty diapers trying to not go crazy around a baby that won't stop crying because it turns out, infants don't give a damn about your need for sleep?

You two might be Netflix compatible, sure. But when it comes down to the nitty-gritty, like debating the real ranking of *Die Hard* movies (which, let's be honest, is a crucial discussion if you want to know who you are actually dealing with here), it's a whole different ballgame. Can you align on the big stuff— like what values you're gonna instill in your mini-me? Are you going to raise a little badass who knows the importance of honesty, resilience, and the undeniable fact that *Die Hard* is, indeed, a Christmas movie?

The quest to find "the one" feels like traveling from one end to the other of hell. One minute you're swiping right; the next you're pondering the existential crisis of parenthood. It's like standing at the edge of a cliff, blindfolded, wondering if you should take the leap. Will she be the Thelma to your Louise, the Bonnie to your Clyde, in this adventure of raising a tiny human who will probably spend the first few years of its life trying to stick forks in sockets and eat dirt? Will she support you in your midlife crisis so you don't go over the edge and go full-on Britney 07?

It's a wild, crazy journey, full of uncertainties and what-ifs. But hey, that's the beauty of it, right? The chaos, the madness, the sheer unpredictability of it all. It's like being on a rollercoaster that's lost its damn mind. And when you finally find that person who's just as crazy and messed up as you are, who's willing to dive headfirst into this beautifully chaotic thing called parenthood—well, that's when you know. You've struck gold, my friend. Now, go forth and creampie it out (or at least practice a lot), and may the odds be ever in your favor.

My brain as a horny fourteen-year-old didn't go as deep into the thoughts of my possible mixed viet/quebecer baby. It pretty much stopped at "Will I get my first blowjob from that girl?" For the record,

I did. We also didn't last long enough for things to get serious. We both shared our first oral sex experiences, watched a few movies together, held hands in front of friends, but eventually like every first-ever boyfriend/girlfriend relationship, it ended because one of us wanted to go toward someone else (it was me; I was the dirtbag in that story). But the inner questioning became more and more complex with each girlfriend I had, especially once I started having actual sex.

Crazy to think that my sexual education was a hodgepodge of Hollywood myths, steamy porn from websites filled with viruses that would make the family computer crash, Google's deep dives through reddit forums, and, well, the less said about my porn-influenced notions of romance, the better. Imagine a curriculum designed by a hormonal teenager with an unlimited data plan and zero supervision from extremely naive parents—that was me.

In the educational wasteland I trudged through, the sum total of "formal" sex ed was a crash course in STDs and a vague notion that a guy plus a gal in the right (or wrong) moment equals baby-making. It was like being handed the keys to a Ferrari after watching a couple of *Fast and Furious* movies. Sure, I knew how to start the engine, but navigating the twists and turns of real relationships? Not a clue.

There I was, a walking, talking embodiment of misguided teen hormones, navigating the dating world with the finesse of a bull in a china shop. The societal script said guys don't ask, don't tell, and definitely don't share feelings. So, I kept all the confusion and questions bottled up, pretending my gut instincts—fueled by a diet of fast food and way too many sugar-filled Red Bulls—were a reliable compass.

But here's the kicker, the real wisdom that would have been gold from dear old dad: the energy exchange in sexual relationships. No one told me that when you sleep with someone, it's not just a physical tangle; you're swapping vibes, moods, and, yes, sometimes their truckload of emotional baggage. Sleeping with a toxic person is like willingly strapping on a backpack full of their junk. You carry it, maybe not realizing at first, but sooner or later, you feel that weight.

Imagine the difference it would have made knowing that each intimate encounter wasn't just a physical conquest or a notch on the bedpost but an exchange of energy, for better or worse. Maybe then I would've been a little pickier, a little wiser, or at least had a better understanding of why I sometimes felt like a human garbage can after a seemingly fun night out with Katrina or Cindy.

Look, when you're a young fuck, roaming around with your pants tenting at every little thing that moves, nobody sits you down for a heart-to-heart about the cosmic dance of the horizontal mambo. It's not just a matter of humping, pumping and dumping, bro. There's a whole spiritual symphony playing in the background when you're balls deep. Every thrust, every moan is like tuning your soul's radio to a higher frequency. And let's be honest, we're talking about a full-body crescendo here, a spiritual eruption that's as scientific as it is mystical. Fuck, that was poetic.

So, you're this high-vibe dynamo, buzzing like a neon sign, and then you hook up with Miss Low-Frequency. It's not just a roll in the hay; it's an energy heist! She's not just after your bodily fluids, homie, trying to suck all of that juice out of the snake; she's siphoning off your top-tier vibes because she's running on empty. It's like a spiritual transaction, but you're getting the raw end of the deal.

Now, let's get real about vibrations. We're not talking about your grandma's back massager. Or these new BaBylissPRO VibeFX massagers that barbers use on your face during hot towel shaves to get some extra tip. We're talking about the kind of vibrations that shape your very being. Putting my science teacher hat on here. Did you know that certain sound frequencies, like those from 60 to 100 Hz, can screw with your head? They crank up anxiety, stir the pot of negative thinking. If a simple tune can mess with your mojo that much, imagine what plunging your magic stick—shoutout to 50 Cent—into a vibe vacuum can do to you. That's some heavy stuff.

But here's the twist: When you find someone who's vibing at your level, who gets your spiritual frequency, sex isn't just sex. It's like a supernova of pleasure. The big O comes knocking like it's got a VIP pass, and let me tell you, it's a whole different ballgame. This kind of connection is rarer than a unicorn with a winning lottery ticket, especially with someone you just met at a bar who probably can't even spell your last name.

And here's why I truly believe that without this insane connection on a higher level, it's almost impossible to get a mini-me done. Even when I was hit by the fatherhood bug at the ripe age of nineteen, none of my girlfriends got the bun in the oven treatment. Even when I was too lay to pull out. Why? Because even though some of them seemed like "The One," our energies were as mismatched as socks on a hungover Sunday. It's all about the cosmic connection, baby.

Man, the relationship I was in when I thought settling down was the next big chapter in my life's messed-up novel was as toxic as a Chernobyl cocktail.

But there I was, Mr. Lovestruck Fool, wearing heart-shaped goggles that made everything look like a goddamn Valentine's card. You know the saying "blinded by love"? Yeah, I cringe just saying it. It's as cliché as those god-awful "Live, Laugh, Love" signs that Karens plaster all over their suburban dungeons like it's some deep philosophical mantra. But, damn it, that's exactly what it was.

This chick, let's call her Miss Radioactive, she had my head spinning faster than a drunk on a merry-go-round. I always thought she was hot when we were in high school but I was too fucking basic to even get any attention from her back then. But when that changed at nineteen years old, I got her, and her toxicity slowly poisoned my blind ass.

Every red flag was just another reason for me to say, "Ah, she's just passionate, you know?" Passionate, my ass! She was like a human hurricane, tearing through my life, leaving a trail of emotional debris.

Truth is I was addicted to the chaos, the roller coaster of highs and lows, mistaking it for some kind of profound love story. In reality, it was just two messed-up people clinging to each other like two drunks trying to walk straight.

During that relationship, Jameson was my closest companion. A full bottle of that sweet, amber nectar would barely last me two days. Picture this: me, sprawled out on a filthy mattress—and I'm talking just a mattress here, no fancy bed frame or anything—with my trusty bottle of whiskey keeping vigil by my side. I'd take a swig, a solid two-ounce hit, every few minutes until the world went fuzzy and I passed out. That was my nightly routine, a lullaby of liquor. Pathetic, isn't it?

Money? What money? Every penny I earned from those $15 haircuts was funneling straight into my whiskey fund and rent for a crappy 1 ½ apartment next to a shady depanneur. Food wasn't even on the budget. I was swiping sandwiches from the local grocery store like a culinary ninja. I'd have five grocery stores of predilections that I'd put on rotation to avoid spending the next couple months in jail.

Professionally, things were looking a bit brighter, though. I'd graduated from bathroom-stall haircuts to renting a room in a local tattoo shop. Cuts & tatts—the concept was badass, a real stroke of genius. It wasn't a world's first but there sure was nothing like it anywhere around me. For a guy who didn't even finish high school—always thought hair school was for edgy girls with star tattoos and eyebrow piercings—I was doing all right. But that's where the good news ended.

My relationship was a dumpster fire. I was the king of cuckolds, a throne I never wanted. A fetish for some, a nightmare for me. She cheated on me with a so-called "friend" while I was touring, and like a lovesick puppy, I stayed with her. Why? Because teenage me had a hardcore crush on her, and now I finally had her. Plus, her family was nice to me, a first in my dating history. Most parents saw me as a tattooed, talentless metalhead going nowhere fast. They weren't wrong, but I wasn't a bad guy either. I was just a little bit lost.

Her folks were already hinting about wanting grandkids. They'd had their kids young (as all farmers do), so the pressure was mounting for their daughters. We weren't using protection; I was too hammered to bother with condoms, and besides, booze felt like a better investment. So there I was, entertaining the thought of settling down with her, imagining farmer babies and a life of domestic bliss. Maybe all the problems in our relationship would just vanish if she got pregnant. Maybe, just maybe, a baby would fix everything.

Deep down, I knew she didn't fit into my fatherhood dream. We never used protection, never pulled out, never tracked a calendar, but nothing happened. It was like the universe itself was telling me, "This ain't it, chief."

Ignoring red flags? It's like a sport for me. But the harsh truth hit me like a ton of bricks—she was unfaithful, jobless, didn't believe in my dreams, but hell, maybe those red flags are there for a reason. Maybe they're not just decorations on the path to self-destruction.

A few months after I mustered the balls to dump her—and let's be clear, it took her giving a blowjob to a dude who looked like Harry Potter if he'd been on a meth binge for me to see the light—she ended up knocked up by some other loser. My buddies were quick to pat me on the back, telling me I'd dodged a bullet. But, honestly, it was more profound than just evading a human train wreck. I started to believe that our failure to reproduce wasn't just bad luck or crappy timing. It was the universe's way of saying, "Wrong frequency, dude."

Think about it: We were like two radios tuned to different stations, never syncing up. That's why she never got pregnant with my kid. It wasn't meant to be. This whole ordeal got me thinking that maybe finding "the one" isn't something you can control. It's like the universe is this cosmic David Getta, and it'll eventually spin a track that matches your beat. You just gotta have faith and let it play out.

Now, what the hell does a "serious relationship" even mean these days? For me, post-Harry-Potter-gate, I reckon I stumbled into just one more "serious" gig before hitting the jackpot with my wife. She's not just my partner; she's the rockstar mother of my kids. That other relationship? It was like the universe's way of giving me a tutorial on what real connection could feel like, a prep course for the main event. Like the previous mistake, I ended up moving in together with this girl but I had my shit together a lot more so there seemed to be hope for this to be the real deal… but not for long.

So there I was, in another "serious" relationship, still playing Russian roulette with my swimmers—no protection, ever. Remember, my old man never gave me the birds and bees chat. The closest thing I got was from a morbidly obese, smelly science teacher I couldn't stand. Like, seriously, who'd even want to imagine that guy getting busy? So, his warnings about STDs and the dangers of pre-cum went in one ear and out the other. I kept saying to myself, "My pull-out game is strong. I'm good."

This chick wasn't the average girl I was usually getting involved with. She wasn't a cheater, had her career and finances sorted, and came from a good family. Picture a goth-preppy hybrid with an air of uptightness—a real prize if that's your thing. But let's be real, the whole thing was doomed from the start. Actually, from the second start. We dated when I was seventeen, and giving it another shot at twenty was like trying to reheat a cold, soggy pizza. It only works out when you're high. And that's exactly why it worked for a little while.

To set the scene, I'd just moved to the big city of Montreal, diving headfirst into a relatively heavy cocaine habit (let's face it, there's no "moderate" use of cocaine; all use of it is abuse). I was grinding twelve-hour days at the barbershop, raking in more cash than I'd ever seen and touched, and for the first time, women were giving me the "let's lick each other's buttholes tonight" kind of look in clubs. Maybe ditching my wolf-print tees and fake Armani glasses for contacts helped, but I was suddenly becoming sort of a Mr. Popular at the bars.

Like I said, we did move in and live together, sure, but there were no grand plans for the future. She wasn't keen on kids (she looked at them like I look at vegans buying Beyond Meat at the store), and I couldn't see myself with someone whose culinary skills peaked at boiling water and who provided less bedroom action than my own left hand.

This relationship was another lesson in cosmic compatibility. When the vibes are off, you can forget about making miracle babies.

Yeah, I know, we all hear those stories—one-night stands leading to pregnancy, toxic couples spawning kids, and then things spiral into a dumpster fire of drama. True, these happen. But I see those as karmic lessons, like the universe doling out life homework. People getting tangled in these messes are just paying their soul's dues. The universe never forgets what you owe.

In my case, it seemed like my karmic debt in the baby-making department was settled. The universe had a big, fat "NO" stamped on any plans to procreate with someone who wasn't destined to be the perfect mother to my kids. It was like there was this cosmic bouncer, blocking any entry into fatherhood until the right woman came along. It's wild how the universe works—kind of like a spiritual matchmaker with a twisted sense of humor, enjoying torturing me a little before giving me who I really need.

Every single one of my past relationships before meeting my wife? Pure karmic payback, man. They were like brutal, no-holds-barred life lessons. Sure, I picked up a trick or two in the bed, gained some confidence in my "how to make them moan louder than an 18-wheeler and squirt harder than Squirtle on steroids" moves, but the real learning was all about me—figuring out my limits, my core values. With every relationship crash and burn, my picture of the ideal baby mama came into sharper focus. Now, looking back with the wisdom of having found "the one," this whole idea of Karmic relationships blows my mind.

Here's what I think this shit is: Karmic relationships are a whole different beast compared to soulmate connections. They're not your smooth-sailing, fairy-tale romances. Oh no, they're like emotional roller coasters on steroids, designed to push every single button you've got. They can and will drive you nuts, and we often slap the "toxic" label on them because, let's face it, they feel like they're poisoning your heart. But that's the point of karma, right? It's like you're settling the score from some past-life drama where you were the villain. Because we're all villains in someone's story at some point and time in this life or a past one.

Now, I'm no enlightened monk from fucking Tibet, and my experience with meth is limited to a couple of wild rides (not enough to fry my brain, thankfully). But from what life's thrown at me, here's my two cents: If you're in tune with your emotions, if you're doing the soul-searching inner work, the universe has a way of handing you the relationships you need exactly when you need them. It's not about endlessly wondering if she's "the one." When it happens, you just know. You feel it in your bones. You feel it in your soul.

That's exactly how it played out with Victoria. It wasn't a question, a doubt, or a puzzle. It was as clear as day. She came into my life and it was like the universe saying, "Here you go, bro. This is what you've been waiting for." It was a connection that transcended all the chaos and craziness of those karmic romances. On top of it, gosh was she hot (still is by the way), but more than anything it was real, it was right, and it just made sense. Like finally finding the missing piece to a puzzle you've been trying to solve your whole life and the puzzle only got you more and more frustrated with yourself as you got older.

The Los Angeles pornstar scene, man, it was a fucking wild ride I never expected to hop on (pun intended). Think about it—a lot of these dudes get their start with foot fetish shit, having to lick some Russian wannabe model's feet on camera, or circle jerk with a couple other desperate homies for some no-name trashy porn production, and there I was, hashtagging #Calipornia like a boss on all my social posts. 2015, that summer was off the fucking rails. I was living large, snorting crushed Adderall like it was candy, gambling with these drunk-as-hell Asian dudes, and doing lines off my girl's giant silicone tits—500cc of pure GGG glory.

And the strip clubs? Jesus, I was chain-smoking like a chimney, getting lap dances paid by my five-foot-two sexbomb that would make a priest blush. But the peak of that madness? Tossing out a couple hundred bucks worth of top-shelf coke to a pair of horny friends gearing up for an orgy in some hotel room in the Hard Rock Hotel in Las Vegas at the AVN awards. Why? Because my barber ass had a flight to catch back to Montreal the next day and I couldn't miss it.

That night in Vegas was batshit crazy, but honestly, that strangely just felt like another Tuesday for me back then. My first five months with Victoria? It was a nonstop, debauched roller coaster. We're talking days, nights, weeks that were a blur of excess and wild shit.

But here's the fucking thing: Amidst all that chaos, there was this surreal sense of trust in the universe. There was no way this was wrong. You know when you just fucking know someone is "the one"? That's what it was like with us. And then, bam! A positive pregnancy test. Just like that, my whole world flipped on its head. One minute I'm living this insane, hedonistic, almost demonic lifestyle, and the next, I'm staring down the barrel of fatherhood. It's nuts how life throws these curveballs at you. But in a way, it felt right, like all the universe's cosmic puzzle pieces finally clicking into place. I had asked for this, I had dreamt of this, and now, it was reality.

Now, gather 'round, kiddos, 'cause it's story time about how I met Victoria. Just like in "how I met your mother." This tale's about how I met Victoria, the Calabasas babe. You know, Calabasas in California, where every trip to the rip-off grocery stores might have you bumping elbows with some Hollywood big-shot while paying $39.99 USD for a pack of pre-cut cucumbers.

The month was June, Victoria was on a little adventure to Montreal to come visit her family and some friends, and we'd been burning up the internet with our continuous sexting—yeah, sexting, lots and lots of it. I finally grew a pair and asked her over to my sick-ass Old Port condo for a date. She said yes, and suddenly, I was sweating bullets. Read it a second time to be sure; yes, she said yes.

My grand seduction plan? To whip up some fancy salmon dinner with roasted potatoes and veggies, all grilled on my rooftop barbecue. Serving this masterpiece on golden plates, paired with my then-favorite wine, Revolution White, a whopping $12 treasure from Couche-Tard. I was no wine connoisseur; all I knew was it took about one and a half bottles to get me singing outside of my shower on Tuesdays.

So, I was jittery as hell. Or if you prefer…freaking the fuck out. Usually, I'm not the "impress 'em at home" guy. More like the "wine and dine 'em at a fancy place with a hook-up" type. But Victoria? THE Victoria. She was different. I was smitten, despite only knowing her digital, pixel-perfect self—every angle, pose, and holes filled if you catch my drift.

Cue the disaster: I torched the salmon, annihilated the potatoes, and turned the veggies into a culinary crime scene. I ain't no Gordon Ramsay, but damn, I outdid myself in kitchen atrocities. On any season of *MasterChef*, I was being eliminated. But hey, I had a solid excuse. The moment Victoria came in, everything else vanished from my thoughts. We dove into conversation, locking eyes, talking about everything and anything—no awkward silences, just pure, electric connection. It was like those whacked-out, coked-up chats about aliens and government spy birds in nightclub bathrooms, but real, raw, and absolutely captivating. My heart was pounding so hard that I was struggling to keep focused on her angel voice.

And just like that, in less than five hours, I was head over heels. The food was toast, the wine was finished, but who cares? I was in love.

So, get this: Only a few wild weeks into dating Victoria, not months or goddamn years, but weeks (Victoria actually confessed to me she remembers the exact time like it was yesterday), I dropped the bomb—I want her to be the mother of my kids. Yeah, I had this dream of being not just any dad, but a freaking superhero of a father, a badass dad, a DADass. I'd thought about it with others before, sure. But not, like, really wanting it. It's like playing with fire, right? You don't plan on burning your dick while drunkenly pissing into a campfire, but you've gotta know where the nearest ER is, just in case.

With Victoria, it was different. Everything was different. I wasn't even shitting bricks or anything telling her. It was like my gut was screaming, "This is the one, you lucky bastard." Our vibes? They were like two perfectly tuned instruments in an orchestra of chaos. Life could hurl whatever crap it wanted at us; I just knew we were destined to have a family together and raise amazing kids.

Now, let's pause for a reality check. She hadn't wanted kids before. She was even married before to some loser-ass English pornstar. Hell, we'd just met, and we weren't even in the same freaking country half the fucking time. And yeah, she was a pornstar—baby-making is pretty much a career killer in that line of work. But guess what? She didn't bolt out the door, buy a pack of smokes, and vanish into the night. Instead, she laughed, said something like, "You're crazy," and then planted one on me. Kissed me with the strength of a thousand waterfalls, like Dwight would say. That's all the confirmation I needed. She was all in, crazy about me, and maybe just a bit crazy herself to trust me to be the father of her kids.

That kiss sealed the deal. It was wild, reckless, and completely batshit insane. But that's how we rolled—fast, furious, and with the subtlety of a sledgehammer. In that moment, I knew we were on a one-way trip to the most chaotic, love-drunk adventure of our lives.

Buckle up, 'cause this ride's about to get even crazier. Yup, it just never stops with this fucking book.

Six months into our whirlwind romance, Victoria was pregnant with our first son, Landon. This was about a month after I kicked my cocaine habit—and by cocaine, I mean that wild cocktail of PCP and God knows what else that we used to snort like there was no tomorrow. Man, I used to love that shit so much I'd drive two hours in traffic for a bump before work.

We found out it was a boy pretty early on with tests, and that's when Victoria dropped a cosmic bombshell on me: Her mom, a retired astrologer whom I'd met once and who was as close to her daughter as a shark is to a goldfish, had decided to speak to her and predicted Victoria would pop out two sons in the near future. This prediction came while Victoria was still shackled to the boozed-up English porn star she'd been trying to ditch without sending him off the deep end. Talk about eerie, right? The guy was so toxic he'd attempt to break her nose in a fight just to turn around and attempt suicide. A pure shit show of a man.

But it ended up being right. We have two amazing boys at home. Both of them are actually playing Legos in front of me as I'm typing this.

But back then, this prediction felt like the universe slapping me in the face with a sign. If you need proof that tapping into some mystical energy can get you what you need, well, there it was, served on a silver platter.

I never doubted my gut. I always knew I'd be a kick-ass dad (a true dadass) and find "The One."

It's like the universe playing matchmaker.

Here's my two cents for all you lost souls out there: Start vibing high, and the universe will sort your love life out. Every fling, every crash and burn, it's all part of the grand plan. And if you're constantly asking, "Is she the one?" then, buddy, you're barking up the wrong tree. When it's right, it's like a runaway train on tracks made of destiny— unstoppable, undeniable, and totally insane. I love you to the moon and back, Victoria.

CHAPTER 3:

BABY IS IN THE OVEN

First time stepping into this bodybuilder gym that's got more testosterone floating around than a bootleg prison bullfighting ring. You know, the type of gym where the machines look like they've been through World War III from all the steroid-filled dudes overusing them as much as they overuse horse medicine to get so jacked they can't fit a standard door.

First things first, I was sneaking into the changing room, ducking into the john like a ninja. Why? To rail two lines of Colombia's finest right off the toilet seat. I was not the only dude using these for illegal stuff; the garbage can was overflowing with used TRT needles. As for me, that's right, I was turning the bathroom stall into my personal pre-workout station. Because, obviously, when you're about as buff as a strand of spaghetti, a little nose candy is just what the doctor ordered, right? Coke head energy.

I was decked out in my finest gym attire—a cut-off The Acacia Strain tour shirt, 'cause nothing screams "I lift, bro" like showing off my tattooed arms that were as muscular as an overcooked butter linguine. And let's not forget the pièce de résistance: black short shorts that were so revealing they were practically giving away a free show of the skinniest thighs on the island of Montreal.

Victoria, man, she's the one who dragged me to this muscle-factory. Her theory? That me tipping the scales at 141 pounds and nearly six feet tall, with muscles that might as well be made of wet tissue paper, wasn't exactly the pinnacle of male health. Einstein had nothing on her.

So, armed with my newfound coke-fueled courage, I strutted over to the bench press like I owned the damn place. In my head, I was a French Arnold Schwarzenegger, about to show these inked-up Russian mobster lookalikes how it's done. Reality check: The bar alone—we're talking no weights, just the bar—felt like it was made of freaking lead. I was trying to unrack this thing, and it was not budging. My arms were shaking like I was trying to lift Thor's hammer. Victoria offered to help out but fuck that, how embarrassing would that be?

Picture this: a twenty-two-year-old me stepping into a bodybuilding gym for the first time ever. It was like a whole new universe where I realized I was the weakest link. As a teen, I was all about sports—a beast offensive soccer scorer, a decent tennis player (thanks to endless ping-pong duels during school lunch breaks with all the other high school rejects). But then, the allure of weed and video games in a dimly lit room trumped running around a field. So, the idea of actually paying to sweat in a gym? Never crossed my mind. It was all about Kush and NHL on Xbox.

But there I was, coked out of my mind, wandering into this gym, looking as lost as a vegan in a butcher shop. I knew the basics—bench presses, squats, the trusty treadmill, and good ol' dumbbells. But then, my eyes landed on these contraptions from another planet.

Like, what in the actual fuck is that thing where you sit and flap your legs open and closed like a damn clam in heat? What is that supposed to train, my inner hoe? And that other machine, where you're pushing up with your shoulders like you're trying to launch yourself to the moon? I was standing there, slack-jawed, clueless, and feeling about as out of place as a nun at a rave.

For Victoria, who'd been a gym rat for years, it was like watching a trainwreck in slow motion. She was cringing as I was trying to make sense of this fitness alien technology.

Turns out, cocaine isn't exactly the secret ingredient to bench-pressing glory. Who knew? Instead of pumping iron, I was there, heart racing like a jackrabbit, sweating like a sinner in church, and oozing the kind of misguided confidence that only comes from snorting your way to stupidity.

Victoria was watching me, probably wondering at what point her life choices led her to this moment.

And I was realizing, as I nearly collapsed under the weight of a barbell that was a third of my body weight, that maybe—just maybe—she was onto something. Maybe snorting my way through life wasn't the fast track to health and fitness. Maybe, just maybe, it was time to ditch the blow and start actually, you know, taking care of myself. If I wanted to see twenty-five, it was time for a change—and not the kind you snort.

Fast forward a bit, and there I was, kicking my drug habits to the curb as Victoria was cooking up our first kid in her belly. Let's be real, if I'd kept nosediving into the white powder, I'd be six feet under instead of writing this masterpiece you can't seem to stop reading. I owe Victoria big-time—she saved not just my sorry ass but also gave me the gift of being a dad. Talk about a wake-up call.

So, at that point, we were hitting the gym together like it was our new religion. Victoria, she was relentless, convinced that pumping iron was my salvation. And there was no way I was letting my pint-sized powerhouse of a wife out-lift me. Picture this: a five-foot-two dynamo who can squat more than her husband weighs. That's not a look I was going for. No, sir, I had to man up, match her stride for stride, rep for rep. I ain't no pussy.

Turns out, sweating it out together was the secret sauce I needed to keep on track and stay motivated. It's like those studies from 2015 and 2021 that said couples who hit the gym together are onto something good. It's not just about getting shredded or looking good in a tank top. It's about pushing each other, growing stronger together, both in muscle and in marriage. It's true; they've proved it.

We weren't always side by side, grunting and lifting. Sometimes it was just about being there at the same time, sharing that space, that commitment. Driving to the muscle temple together. It's like our relationship got a steroid shot—in a good way. Healthier bodies, happier minds, and a connection that's rock solid.

Victoria, throughout her entire pregnancy, she was hitting the gym with me every day like it owed her money. Morning sickness? She laughed in its face. Back pain? More like a minor inconvenience.

Sensitive nipples? She just powered through. There she was, waddling into the gym, belly and all, making every excuse-making gym rat look like little babies on leg day.

You've heard those wild stories, right? About moms lifting cars off their kids, tapping into some insane, hidden mom strength brought to them by the power of motherhood? Well, pregnancy must've unlocked Victoria's version of that. It was like watching Wonder Woman in action, only more badass because it's real life and she's my fucking wife. She was lifting, squatting, and sweating up a storm, all while sporting a baby bump that kept on getting bigger and heavier by the day. It was nothing short of inspiring and hella motivating.

But let me tell you, as her belly got bigger, things got weirder. Gym bros, you know the type—guys usually too busy flexing in the mirror to notice anything else—started doing double-takes. It's like they'd never seen a pregnant woman before, especially not one who could probably out-lift them. They started acting creepy as hell.

The gym turned into a freak show the bigger Victoria's belly got. Random girls, who wouldn't know her from Eve, suddenly became belly-rubbing fanatics. No respect for personal space. They were flocking to her like she was some mystical Buddha, rubbing her bump as if it were going to grant them three wishes. It's like they thought pregnancy was contagious and they were trying to catch it through osmosis. Yeah, invasive as fuck.

And the dudes, oh man, the dudes. You've got these acne-ridden, steroid-pumped guys acting like knights in shining armor, offering to spot her on machines that were literally designed to eliminate the need for a spotter. If I wasn't around, it wouldn't take a minute before one of them airheads ran up to her. It was like watching moths drawn to a flame—except the flame was my pregnant wife and the moths were gym bros with more testosterone than sense.

But the creepiest of them all? This one takes the cake. I swear to god it went just like this: Victoria finished her set on the bench, walked off to grab a sip of water at the water fountain, and in swooped

Mr. Clean's evil twin—this massive, bald dude with more veins on his biceps than ripples in the ocean. He made a beeline for the bench and...I kid you not, started sniffing it like a bloodhound on a scent. Not in disgust ,no, with the biggest fucking smile on his face. I'm talking full-on nostrils flared, deeply inhaling the essence of "Eau de Pregnant Wife." It's like something out of a horror movie, only you can't look away because it's happening right in front of you.

Seven months into the pregnancy, and this wasn't our first rodeo with weirdos anywhere we went. Seems like there was something about pregnant women that flipped a switch in some guys. Was it science? Was it just because Victoria was rocking that pregnancy glow like a supermodel? Turned out, it was a bit of both. Men get weird, and yeah, my wife is smoking hot, even with a baby on board.

All right, buckle up, my man, because when your lady starts showing off that baby bump, you're about to witness some seriously bizarre behavior. I dove headfirst into this research, and what I found was straight-up mindfuckingblowing. So I found this study from 2011 in Europe that laid it all out: The more a guy is around his mom being pregnant or breastfeeding as a little chaos-maker (ages one to five), the higher the chances he's gonna find pregnant women or breastfeeding moms kinda hot. Yeah, really, that's not even fake. No wonder the "Stepmom" porn category is so popular.

We're talking 66 percent of these guys, especially the older siblings, having been front row and center to mommy's maternity show. This isn't just some random shit that happens to born weirdos only; it's rooted in a term science calls "sexual imprinting." Sounds like something out of a wildlife documentary, right? But it's real. This process basically scripts your future attractions and mate choices, all based on good ol' mom.

So, if you were hanging around mom while she was knocked up or nursing your baby bro or sis, guess what? Pregnancy might just be your thing, and you probably didn't even realize it until you were old enough to vote. Childhood, man, it's a trip.

But wait, there's even more to this strange phenomenon. Freud had this "oedipal phase" theory—you know, kids being in love with their opposite-sex parent and all that jazz. Turns out, there's a bit of overlap with this whole sexual imprinting thing. Who knew? Wifey has to be like mommy.

And get this: some of these dudes are also into pregnant women because of primal instincts—like jealousy and competition. It's like they see a pregnant woman and think, "Ah, a fertile mate! Must protect, must compete!" Caveman brain, 21st century edition.

Welcome to the wild ride of "baby mama is pregnant" territory. It's a trip that is filled with weirdness and mixed emotions, let me tell you. With this chapter, my mission is to lay it all out for you— the good, the bad, the scary, the "what the fuck is happening," and the downright batshit crazy. If you're about to embark on this journey, that should prepare you mentally. And if you've been there, done that, and felt like you were about as useful as a chocolate teapot during the whole thing, you'll feel less alone, brother.

But hey, don't start drowning in self-pity just yet. This chapter isn't just about the freak show you're about to witness and all the emotions that come with it; it's also about shining a light on the unsung hero of pregnancy: the future dad. That's right, you. You might feel like you're just the guy who provided the initial spark, the seed, but trust me, you're way more than that.

We future dads, we've got a backstage pass to the whole pregnancy show. And yeah, it might feel like we're just the supporting act, but we're playing a crucial role. Even Metallica needs a support act; that's solid proof that the gig is important. Your journey to badass dad kicks off the second that pregnancy test shows a positive. No more rehearsals, no more "I'll figure it out later." It's game time, and you gotta step up to the plate like a fucking legend.

You need to morph into the best damn version of yourself, pronto. We're talking about being Mr. Reliable, Mr. Supportive, Mr. "I Got This"—all rolled into one dude. The minute that test turns positive, you're not just some dude; you're a dad-in-the-making, and it's your job to be the rock for your baby mama.

First of all, let's cut through the BS and talk about the giant pink and blue elephant in the room: pregnant sex. Man, when Victoria was pregnant, it's like every guy at the barbershop suddenly turned into a perverted sex therapist with a one-track mind. "How's pregnant sex, bro?" they'd ask with this look in their eye, pupils the size of Mount Everest, like they're about to uncover the secrets of the universe.

It's a fucking weird mix. Some of these dudes are practically drooling at the thought. They've got this fantasy where a pregnant woman, with her belly and all, is the pinnacle of sex appeal. They're picturing it as some kind of erotic Nirvana, like they've stumbled onto the holy grail of kinks. They almost get hard just thinking about it so they have to know all the details so they can fantasize about it later with their left hand and a box of Kleenex.

Then there's the other camp. These guys are scared shitless. They're imagining some horror movie scenario where every thrust is like poking the baby's forehead. They've got this twisted idea that sex with a pregnant woman is like navigating an uncomfortable minefield, where one wrong move could spell disaster.

But the truth is kind of disappointing, in my opinion. You might be hoping for some wild, mind-blowing stories that sound like they're straight out of a steamy romance novel. Some *Fifty Shades of Grey* type of shit. But I'm gonna burst that bubble right now. The truth? It's pretty...normal. Yeah, a bit of a letdown for the rumor mill.

For the first five, maybe even six months, it's business as usual. Some women don't even start showing a baby bump until the fifth month, so physically, things aren't all that different from your pre-pregnancy romps. Okay, boobs might be slightly bigger so if you're a boob man, you'll dig that part for sure. But the fireworks aren't exactly exploding in new colors, if you catch my drift.

The only thing, though—the plot twist if you will, and that's not for all of them but it happened to my wife—the hormonal roller coaster sends baby mama's libido into overdrive. We're talking first and second trimester here, science proves it; her hormones are doing the cha-cha slide, and suddenly, she's got the sex drive of a teenage boy whose only plan for the day is to set a new personal record in the art of jerking off.

So, while the mechanics of the act don't change much (unless you have a kinky baby mama who loves to try new kinky stuff), the frequency? That's a whole different ballgame. Get ready. It's like she's tapped into this wellspring of horniness, and you're suddenly trying to keep up with this newfound appetite that she has for your dick. It's a mix of exhilarating and exhausting, like trying to keep pace with a marathon runner when you're used to slow morning jogs with your dog.

So, does the horny train ever pull into the station? You bet it does. Once you pass the six-month mark, things start to shift back to "normal," or at least what passes for normal in the land of pregnancy. Why the change? Well, hormones are still running the show, but now there's a new headliner: The belly is usually fucking round and huge. That growing baby bump turns into the ultimate cockblock, making sex about as comfortable as a sumo wrestler would be in a Smart car.

That's why when those nosy, pervy dudes at the barbershop grilled me about pregnant sex, my answers were pretty grounded. Sure, it's great for a good stretch, if you already have a great sex life, then it hits a bit of a snag. You find yourself limited to the basics, the old faithful positions, mostly doggy to be honest, because let's face it, maneuvering around a baby bump isn't exactly a walk in the park. There's no more putting her legs behind her head or twitting her in all sorts of ways so you can hit deeper.

But here's the real deal: If you're into your lady, like you should, and if you've got a healthy sex life pre-baby on board, then pregnant sex isn't going to throw you for a loop. It's like your regular routine with a few curveballs thrown in. Nothing that makes it horrible. For me, it was a godsend. The last thing I needed during those nine stressful roller coaster months was to start sweating bullets every time sexy time rolled around.

Why stressful, you might ask? Well there's something that you, as a future dad, play a key role in that isn't always easy to manage and it comes at you like a swarm of bees—relentless and fucking often during these whole nine months: checkup appointments.

They're supposed to be reassuring, a way for your doctor to keep tabs on everything that's going down in baby town. Sounds great, right? In theory, oh yeah, sure. It's like having a direct line to the pregnancy gods, who are supposed to know everything, a chance to unload every worry, question, and weird Google search result you've come across in the last few weeks.

But here's the cold, hard truth: For most of us diving into this baby-making enigma for the first time, our knowledge about what's happening inside a woman's body during pregnancy is about as vast as a water puddle in the Sahara. The list of questions we have is longer than a cross-country ski trip from Ottawa to Edmonton. It's overwhelming, and more often than not, these appointments build up a fuckload of anxiety.

As a future dad, you walk into these appointments with your head spinning. "Is the baby growing right? What's that weird pain she says she has? Can she eat sushi? Isn't her purse too heavy for her to carry? Why is she crying over *The Office*?" It's an endless stream of confusion and concern for your lady. You're supposed to be the supportive, got-it-all-figured-out partner, but inside, you're more like a lost kid in a Walmart.

You're already juggling your own anxiety like a circus clown with too many balls of fire in the air. But wait, there's more. Your baby mama, the one actually carrying this tiny human inside her, your mini-me, is on a whole other level of stress. And let's be real, she's got questions—as she fucking should.

Every appointment is like walking a tightrope for her. She's wracked with worry, thinking maybe she ate something wrong, did something she shouldn't have, and now the doc's gonna drop the "unfit mother" bomb on her. It's like watching a pressure cooker ready to blow.

But here's where you, future dadass, have to come into play. It's your job, your mission, to not let her spiral down that rabbit hole of panic and guilt as she's buckling up in the car on the way to the appointments. She's already doing the heavy lifting, literally, so the last thing she needs is to be drowning in "what ifs" and "should haves" every time the doctor wants to check up on her.

We might be hella clueless as newbie fathers, about as savvy as a goldfish on a bicycle, but if there's one thing we can all agree on, it's this: stress is the enemy. It's bad news for mom, bad news for the baby, bad news all around.

No matter how stressed you are, you have to put a brave face on for her. Fake it if you have to but you need to be the calm in the storm, the voice of reason in the whirlwind of worry. You're there to reassure her, to remind her that she's doing a kickass job, to keep those stress levels at bay.

Sure, stepping up and being the protector sounds easy enough, but when the rubber meets the road (new expression I learned last week; glad I was able to throw it in here), it's a whole different ballgame. We guys, we've got that protector instinct hardwired in us, sure. It kicks in almost automatically, raw and primal, especially when our lady and unborn kid are in the picture. But those prenatal appointments? They can throw curveballs that'll knock you right off your fucking feet. Shit you've never seen coming.

I must've drank what felt like my fourth or maybe sixth vodka soda of the night, in under two hours. Dinner at home was this eerie silent black and white mime movie—just me, Victoria, and the buzz of a damn fly doing kamikaze dives at the crystal chandelier on top of our heads. We weren't mad at each other; hell, I almost wish we were. At least then there'd be some noise, some action, some make-up sex and some distraction from the heavy air hanging over us.

We'd just come back from one of those critical, late-stage checkups. The kind where you're so close to the finish line you can almost taste it. Up until then, I'd been Mr. Cool, Calm, and Collected on the outside, always there to pressure her and act like everything was going to be all right. But that appointment? It shattered my cool facade like a sledgehammer through my shin.

I remember watching the nurse, her face all scrunched up in confusion as she glided that ultrasound wand over Victoria's big, round belly. There's our little Landon on the screen, looking like he's just chilling in his private pool. I'm usually tearing up of joy at these moments, like an overly sentimental fool. But not this time.

The nurse's expression was throwing me off. I was making up stories in my head—maybe she's daydreaming about her dinner plans. Is it going to be the microwavable steak and potatoes or the pre-cooked frozen burrito from four days ago? Or maybe she was thinking about that guy she gave a blowjob to in the back of a taxi last week. Will he ever call back? You hear about these nurses pulling insane shifts, like eighteen hours and ten days in a row, so maybe she's just fried, right? But deep down, I knew. I knew something was off.

The doctor walked in, and let me tell you, up until then, our appointments with her were as exciting as watching golf on TV. Routine stuff—weight's good, vitals are all green, baby's doing backflips or whatever in there. It was always in-and-out, with her dishing out those cookie-cutter responses and scribbling out a prescription for those prenatal vitamins like she was on autopilot.

But this time? It was like we stepped into a whole different movie, and I'm not sure I liked the director's cut. She rolled in on her fancy leather chair, slapped on her reading glasses, and started eyeing those ultrasound screenshots like they were some kind of cryptic code. My heart was thumping so loud, I swear it was echoing off the walls. What the fuck is going on?

Beside me, Victoria was a bundle of goddamn nerves. I could feel her stress levels rising as she got so sweaty that her hand on mine felt as if she had just taken a dip with Flipper. The silence in that room was deafening, every tick of the clock a hammer to my brain. *Can you just tell us what the hell is going on?*

The room's air was already thick with tension, as thick as a Latina dancer's ass in a reggeaton music video, and then she dropped the bombshell, the kind of words that you don't want to hear ever: "There's an anomaly with your baby that we are now seeing on these new scans." It was like time froze. Every other sound faded away, and those words just echoed in your head. Anomaly…anomaly…anomaly…

I glanced over at Victoria. Her eyes, brimming with tears, were a mirror of the fear and uncertainty I felt. My gut reaction? I wanted to go full Hulk mode, flip the damn desk, let out a primal roar, and punch holes in the walls—anything to release this tidal wave of emotion crashing over me. But what did I do? I wrapped my arm around her, pulled her close, planted a kiss on her forehead. Because sometimes, that's all you can do. I felt powerless.

The doctor kept talking, her voice a distant hum as she explained "duplex kidney." It sounded like a death sentence, but as she went on, it turned out it was not the end of the world. Most kids with this condition lead totally normal lives. Worst case? A bit more prone to urinary infections. Should be manageable, right?

But there we were, two young, soon-to-be parents, our minds racing a mile a minute, tumbling down the rabbit hole of "what ifs." Our brains weren't hearing "it's manageable." All we were processing was "anomaly," "condition," "problem." We were picturing our little Landon's life turning into some medical drama, filled with challenges and struggles. We were freaking the fuck out.

We were already in that dark place, drowning in worry, sadness gripping us like a vise. All we wanted in that moment was to escape, to get the hell out of that clinical, cold office, away from the words that had turned our world upside down.

We didn't ask questions, didn't probe for more details. We just thanked her and left.

It was just me and Victoria, lost in our own whirlwind of thoughts, each one darker than the last. It led us there, sitting at dinner, staring at those two perfectly cooked filet mignons, but it might as well have been cardboard for all we cared.

Post-dinner, those vodka sodas started doing their magic. Not the "drown your sorrows" kind, but the "let's lighten this mood" kind. Victoria stepped out of the shower, and there I was, suddenly turned stand-up comedian. I started riffing about our little "mutant" Landon, painting him as this superhero whose duplex kidney was his superpower. I was going all out—imagining him sucking venom out of snakebite victims, drinking polluted ocean water to save the planet. It was ridiculous, absurd, and exactly what we needed.

She was laughing, for the first time since we left that doctor's office. It's like those jokes, as dumb as they were, were the pressure valve releasing all that built-up tension. We needed that moment of absurdity to snap us back to reality, to see things as they really were—manageable, not the end of the world.

Looking back, older, wiser me, the Oliver currently writing this book, would've handled the whole situation differently, more maturely, and definitely without the help of alcohol. But I've got to hand it to my younger self—in that moment, he did exactly what a future dadass is supposed to do. He took a crappy situation and turned it around. He found a way to bring back the laughter, to lighten the load, to remind us both that we were going to be okay.

That's what being a dadass is all about. It's not just about being strong and steady; sometimes, it's about being the stupid clown.

Let's face it: Humor is like a Swiss Army knife in the world of relationships, especially during pregnancy. Throughout both of Victoria's pregnancies, my knack for cracking jokes, even the worst kind, even the ones so dark I can't publish them anywhere, was like a lifeline. It's like that old saying, "If you can make a woman laugh, you can make her do anything." In this case, it's more like, "If you can make her laugh, you can help her through anything,"

We dudes, we've got this innate ability to use humor as a shield and a sword. In relationships, we're the savior of heavy moments with jokes always dumber than the last.

But let me lay down some gospel truth about humor during pregnancy. There's one line I never crossed and you shouldn't either: making cracks about weight gain and body changes. Look, I might be as self-conscious about my dad bod as the next guy. Does that make me a bit of a little bit? Possibly. I mean, I'm always hustling to look like a snack for my wife, not just some dude who's let himself go. I'm not aiming for just a twinkle in her eye when I strut into a room; I'm going for full-blown pussy-dripping effect, fireworks explosions, like her vagina is throwing a New Year's Eve party in Niagara Falls because I just showed up. And she's on the same page. It's kind of magical, actually—keeping that flame burning hotter than a redneck backyard barbecue, even after years of seeing each other in all our glorious naked bodies. It's about staying sexy for your partner, even when life throws you two kids, a pair of drooling dogs, and enough room-clearing farts to make you want to stay ten feet away from each other at all times.

But look, when it came to pregnancy cravings, and believe me it's not just a rumor, they do get real weird with some foods, and weight gain. I knew Victoria wasn't going to go off the rails and start inhaling everything in sight, dive headfirst into a pool of junk food and come out on the other side unrecognizable by month eight. She's got this discipline about her, like a ninja with a calorie counter. In a good way, though, not the paranoid type. But hey, let's be real: not everyone's got that control. For some moms-to-be, it's a hormonal roller coaster that turns eating habits upside down. Some people just associate food with emotions, and since pregnancy is a fucking roller coaster of the latter, well, shit gets out of control, and fast. I'm not here to throw shade at anyone who packs on the pounds during pregnancy. I'd never fat shame a pregnant woman. Sometimes, it's just the body doing its wild, hormonal thing. And that's okay, because nothing is irreversible.

But here's the thing for us future dadasses: our job is to be the ultimate hype man during this whole baby-growing saga. You've got to make your lady feel like she's still the queen of your world, no matter how her body is changing. She's transitioning into MILF category, and it's on you to help her feel every bit the part. Even if that means developing a fetish for these swollen ankles and cum on theme once in a while, you gotta do what you gotta do.

Even if your woman is like mine, staying active and fit throughout the pregnancy, there's going to be some body image battles. It's normal and it's okay. Maybe it's her face swelling up like a balloon, or her arms getting a bit chunkier. That's where you step in with your A-game. You've got to be there, telling her she's as hot as ever. It's about keeping it light, fun, and always reaffirming. Just reverse the roles in your head for a second. Imagine carrying a human being in your belly and because of it, you can't control your weight gain and you get so big for a while that you can't see your dick anymore. You'd need moral support, right?

So let's talk about steering the ship right. A real man, a certified dadass in the making, guides his baby mama toward staying healthy, both during and after pregnancy. It's not just about looking good; it's about longevity, setting a good example for the little ones.

I decided to make a list—the Dos and Don'ts for keeping your lady on the healthy track during pregnancy:

- DO encourage her to keep hitting the gym, at her own pace, of course. Get creative with it.

Sync up your workouts; ditch the exercises she can't do and adapt to her. Maybe rename the exercises to add a little humor. Become the gym clown. "Overhead baby press," "baby hammer curl," "baby back row"—you get the idea. Act as if dumbbells are babies. It's stupid, but it lightens the mood and makes working out pregnant more fun. Working out is crucial for her energy, mood, and hormone balance. Plus, it'll make bouncing back post-pregnancy a whole lot smoother. You got this, bro.

- DON'T, for the love of all that's holy, crack jokes about her face getting round and calling her "Moonface." "Good morning, Moonface" is a no go. Trust me. That's a one-way ticket to the doghouse. A lot of women get that puffy, water-retention look in their faces during pregnancy. It's temporary, it passes, and your job is to bite your tongue and remember that if you can't say something nice, don't say anything at all.

- DO open up that wallet and splurge on clothes that make your lady feel like the goddess she is, even if she's only going to wear them for a few months and then never look at them again for the rest of her life. Yeah, I'm talking about shelling out for maternity wear that might cost an arm and a leg and will be practically useless post-pregnancy. But trust me, it's worth every penny. The last thing you want is to find your partner in tears every morning, wrestling with her pre-pregnancy jeans like they're her arch-nemesis. Watching her try to button up jeans that clearly have no intention of cooperating is like watching a tragedy unfold in slow motion. It's heart-wrenching, and you're there, feeling like a helpless bystander. So, what do you do? You invest in her happiness. You buy those clothes that make her feel beautiful, comfortable, and confident. We're not just talking function here; we're talking mental health, self-esteem, the whole nine yards.

- DON'T ever think about calling her out on her mood swings. Yeah, hormones during pregnancy can be an absolute bitch, turning your baby mama into a mood-swinging, tear-jerking, anger-bursting roller coaster—it's like living with a hormonal Godzilla in his prime. It's overwhelming, uncontrollable, and, frankly, a bit terrifying at times. The last thing she needs is some wise-ass holding up a mirror to her face, pointing out how she's flying off the handle over the brand of peanut butter before too spicy or crying over a diaper commercial's lack of realism. Your job, my friend, as a future dadass, is to be the superhero in this hormonal apocalypse—lift her up, don't stand there puffing your chest like you're some kind of saint who never screws up. Pregnancy is not just about bringing a mini-you into the world; it's a crash course in how to handle the crappiest situations with grace. Help her navigate through her feelings but let her control the ship. Don't act like you know best. It's about understanding and supporting your lady, not pointing fingers—unless you're directing her to the nearest ice cream store.

The list of "don'ts" when dealing with your pregnant queen could stretch longer than a CVS receipt after an emergency trip to stop the never ending diarrhea from a bad sushi experience. Seriously, I could've written an entire epic saga titled "What NOT to Do to Your Baby Mama During Pregnancy" and it would rival the length of Dadass for sure. Seriously, it'd be a veritable encyclopedia of pregnancy faux pas, complete with illustrations of dudes getting smacked in the face by a fish (never underestimate pregnancy strength by the way) for saying the wrong thing at the wrong time. Who knows, maybe one day, when I'm not dodging Lego landmines in my house anymore and I have the time to write another successful book, I'll muster up the energy to do it. But honestly, if you've got half a brain and paid even a smidgen of attention to what I've been spouting here in this fucking chapter, you might just get the big picture. It's not rocket science, bro.

The big takeaway from this whole pregnancy experience for a dad-to-be? Pregnancy is a wild, unpredictable ride, full of highs, lows, and a million moments in between. It's a time when you gotta channel your inner Masculine Sacrado. Yeah, it sounds fancy, but it's an age-old concept, steeped in spirituality and tradition. It's about embracing those classic gender roles, but not in some outdated, "back in my day" kind of way.

Now, don't get me wrong. I'm not preaching about living like we're stuck in the 1920s. The modern world has reshaped gender roles in some fantastic ways, bringing equality and respect to the forefront, and I'm all for that. But when it comes to pregnancy, there's something undeniably primal and natural about it, and our role as men has stood the test of time. We're the protectors, the caretakers, the steady hand in the storm.

This isn't just about being physically present. It's deeper than that. It's emotional. It's spiritual. You're the go-to guy for comfort, for support, for everything your lady needs during this intense, life-changing journey.

No matter what your life looks like, no matter how smooth or rocky the pregnancy road is, your role is crystal clear. You're the anchor, the safe harbor in whatever storm comes your way. And that's not a responsibility to take lightly. It's your first real test as a dad, your chance to show the world—and yourself—what you're made of.

So, future dads, wear that role with pride. Never for a second think you're just a bystander in this pregnancy saga. Sure, there'll be times when you feel out of your depth, clueless, maybe even useless. But if you're there, if your heart's in it, trust me, you're doing exactly what's needed.

Being a part of this journey, being there for your partner and your unborn child, that's what sets you apart. That's what forges you into a dadass, long before you ever hold that baby in your arms.

CHAPTER 4:

BYE-BYE FREEDOM

So, my alarm screeches at 6:33 a.m.—yeah, you read that right, 6:33, not 6:30. Why? 'Cause I'm that guy who thinks setting alarms at odd numbers is less of a mind-fuck. Imagine, it's 6:30, you're groggily slapping the snooze button, fumbling for your glasses, yanking out your earplugs (a habit I picked up to drown out the symphony of dudes jerking off and moans from random chicks my bandmates would bring back on the bus at an impossible hour on tour—nothing like the sound of desperate self-love to gross porn and strangers' orgasms to give you PTSD). And then, bam! It's 6:32 and you feel like you've already screwed the day.

But 6:33? That's my jam. It's weirdly precise, like a wink from the universe saying, "Yeah, you're a bit off, but so what?" By the time I'm up and it's 6:36, I'm like, "Cool, still on this oddball schedule." Typing this out, I realize I might be some kind of weirdo sometimes, but hey, who's judging?

And don't even get me started on white plastic shower walls. I can't touch them. They've been the bane of my existence since I was knee-high to a grasshopper. Something about them screams, "I'm a breeding ground for every germ known to man." Might as well touch a needle found in the crackhead park. That aversion hasn't changed a bit since I became a dad. But getting up at the ass-crack of dawn? That's new. Kids, man. They turn your life upside down, shake out all the loose change, and leave you wondering how the hell you got here. But honestly, I wouldn't trade it for the world—or a sane wake-up time.

I reckon most dudes are more petrified at the idea of losing their so-called freedom than actually sucking at being a dad. It's like this primal fear is etched in our DNA, passed down from our cave-dwelling, mammoth-hunting ancestors. Let's zoom back a few thousand years, back when our forefathers were these badass nomadic hunter-gatherers. This was way before anyone thought of farming or conjuring up some cancerous, testosterone-killing, vote-for-the-Liberals veggie patty owned by a tech nerd.

Back then, men were the OG badasses, roaming the wilds sometimes for weeks at a time, spearing the wildest of animals, and dragging their bloody carcasses back home for the whole fam to feast on. Women did their bit too, obviously, but they stuck closer to the camp, the home, keeping the fires burning and the kiddos from getting eaten by saber-toothed tigers or whatever insanely badass animals were walking the earth back then.

Fast forward to yesterday. I'm sneaking out for a peaceful ten-minute phone call about some graphic design gig—a far cry from wrestling with a frickin' bison. And what happens? The second I hang up, I'm yanked back into the domestic jungle by my wife. Mission: Wrestle a tiny human into a dinosaur T-shirt he's decided is his arch-nemesis for the day.

Yeah, life's a bit different now. No more foraging in the wild for days, having some alone time; now it's all about fiddling with fonts and colors in Photoshop to pay for groceries. And let's be real, the only bison I'd be lifting is a bison burger, and that's pushing it. My steroid days at twenty-three were all for the 'gram, not for hauling mammoth-sized game. I actually gained a fuck ton of weight on roads, but it was mostly water retention and I've lost thirty since anyways.

Here's the thing, though: We still harp on about needing our "freedom." Freedom from what? Changing nappies? Helping with homework? Man, it's time to evolve. We're not in the Stone Age anymore. Sure, our inner caveman might grumble about the good ol' days of hunting and gathering, but let's face it, being a modern-day dad is about swapping the spear for a spatula and the hunting grounds for the playground. And honestly, it's a pretty sweet trade. Y'all rather die an atrocious death around age twenty-four or die comfortably in your La-Z-Boy watching *The Office* for the 24,736th time while eating Subway at eighty-seven years old? Choice seems easy…bring me the remote.

So let's take a moment to break it down, shall we? What the hell do men nowadays even consider "freedom"? Seriously, most of us couldn't catch a pig if it was napping, let alone in one of those batshit-crazy pig-chasing contests I used to see at my hometown's summer agriculture exposition. Our hunting skills are about as sharp as a spoon. So, where do we find that elusive sense of freedom? Is it in holing up in our mancaves, glued to *Call of Duty*, surrounded by more tech than NASA in 1995? Or maybe what we consider freedom is even more stupid. Maybe it's hitting the bars, getting so plastered that the barmaid, a solid 4 out of 10, suddenly looks like a double-dose of hotness, leading to almost duking it out with the bouncer and a lost-car-keys fiasco?

Or perhaps, it's flexing in the gym mirror for three hours, ignoring everything but chest and biceps because there's no one at home waiting for you to help with anything remotely resembling responsibility?

I'm gonna lay it out for you. No BS. If you're aiming for that "World's Best Dad" mug, all that crap's gotta go. Yeah, all of it. I'll admit, I clung to some of my "freedom rituals" like a lifeline when I first got slapped with the dad label. And it wasn't a piece of cake to get rid of shitting selfish habits, but as I aged like a fine, slightly sour wine, I realized something. Being there for my family, actually being present and not just physically loafing around, beats the hell out of guzzling cheap beer at some dingy metal show, reminiscing about the "good ol' days" with buddies I barely know anymore.

Don't get it twisted; I'm not here to sound the dad-life death knell. Reading this, you might think turning into a dad means kissing your own life goodbye, becoming nothing more than a diaper-changing, bedtime-story-reading drone. Hell no. Stick with me till the end of this chapter, and you'll see it's the exact opposite. Being a good dad doesn't mean you evaporate into thin air; it means reshaping that sense of freedom into something a hell of a lot more fulfilling.

Let's get real here. I'm five-foot-ten (okay, nearly five-eleven, but I dropped five-ten-and-a-half bit when I realized it made me sound like a fucking toddler bragging about being a "big boy"). My vertical leap? It's laughable. Maybe it's 'cause I'm white and French (let's be honest, it's a stereotype for a reason), or maybe my legs are just decorative since I'm also no Usain Bolt. Either way, I'm about as adept at basketball as a penguin is at flying. In high school, even in those boys vs. girls gym classes, I was picked after the kid who sniffed glue.

The only thing I might have in common with pro basketball players? Dick size. But hand me five vodka sodas at the local hipster bar, and suddenly I'm Michael freakin' Jordan at the arcade hoops. High scores? Demolished. All fueled by the magic combo of booze and a little something-something from Mr. Baggy in my pocket and good old Volvo keys.

My nightlife? It was epic. When I was single, it was all about those high-energy clubs and arcade bars. Arrive at midnight and leave at 3. Married life? Picture this: fancy-ass restaurants, champagne, and bathroom escapades worthy of a seedy sextape that could generate a couple thousand if we had an OnlyFans account. This wasn't just for kicks; it was my lifestyle as one of the coolest barbers in town. Yeah, I owned seven barbershops, snipped the hair of the rich and fabulous, and was hitched to the hottest pornstar on the planet. Money was like confetti, and I threw it like I was at a never-ending pride parade. I never tallied up my weekly party budget, but trust me, it dwarfed what I now spend on diapers and baby food.

To any young dudes out there, this might sound like the ultimate freedom. You're out of the parental nest, no curfews, nobody to answer to. Booze, babes, and bad decisions at your fingertips. It's what I call the "wild phase" of early adulthood. You've been caged up with rules and suddenly you're the master of your own universe, flush with cash and craving freedom like it's oxygen.

But let's peel back that veneer. What I've described? It's not freedom; it's hangovers waiting to happen, a gallery of regrettable choices, and a whole lot of running away from reality. And here's where it gets deep. If you haven't done your shadow work, dealt with the demons and the transgenerational issues, you're just playing dress-up in a suit of escapism.

Now, you're stepping into fatherhood, or maybe you're already knee-deep in it. It's time to redefine freedom. It's not about running wild and unchecked. It's about facing and slaying your inner demons for the greater good. It's about understanding your responsibilities, embracing them, and finding liberation in the things that truly matter. True freedom is about breaking the chains of your own immaturities and stepping up. It's realizing that the wildest adventure isn't in a bar or at the end of a line of white powder. It's in those little faces looking up at you, expecting you to be their hero. That, my friend, is freedom in its purest, most terrifying, and exhilarating form.

Look, I ain't exactly been poster material for "Dad of the Year," and hell, I'm still fumbling through this self-improvement stuff daily. But, you know what? In the past few years, I've been diving headfirst into the world of meditation, breathing (like real breath work), and popping soul-tickling mushrooms in some intense life-changing ceremonies. It's all about hammering my insides into something better—mostly for being a badass dad, but hey, a bit for my own damn sanity too. How can I be the best me for my kids if I don't do the work, right? Later in this book, I'll dive into what these psychedelic ceremonies did for me.

But first, let me tell you this about what most new dads call "freedom."

One day, like a spiritual slap to the face, it hit me: what freedom really means. Spoiler alert: It's all about letting shit go. Forgiveness, man—it's like the VIP pass to the freedom fest.

So, here's the deal: We're cranking up the spiritual stuff in this chapter. Strap in, light a freakin' incense stick (or whatever floats your boat), dim those lights till they're moodier than a teenager's bedroom, suck in a lungful of air, pop your mind wide open, and let's ride this mystical wave. It's about to get deep, funny, and just a tad unhinged—the best kind of soul journey to figure out what freedom now means to me, and maybe what deep down it truly means to you.

Man, let's get real. You've been shooting the love juice since forever, right? Pumping out billions of those little swimmers like it's nothing. And then, bam! The universe, in its infinite, freaky wisdom, picks one—just one—of those wriggly dudes at the exact freakin' moment to crash the party in a woman's body. And not just any woman, oh no. She's the cosmic chosen one, destined to be the mother of your kid. Talk about an energetic mind-bender! You and her, just pawns in the grand scheme of things. Suddenly, you're a dad. Life's flipped upside down, whether you're ready or not, scared shitless or not, planned or not.

That moment you find out you're gonna be a father, something inside you shifts. You might not even notice it, but it's there. It's like shedding your old skin, man. Goodbye to the days of reckless living, pissing away cash, and dancing with self-destruction at wild parties. Say adios to the crutches of drugs, the empty hookups, the running away from your own freaking shadows. All those toxic joys? They gotta go. But the truth is, to truly feel ready to become the best version of yourself, you gotta forgive yourself for all that jazz. It's like spiritual laundry, cleaning out the crap to make space for something way bigger.

Now, let's face the grim reaper for a sec. Before dadhood, death felt like a distant cousin, always there but never too close. Life was about you, your whims, your desires. Even the sucky parts, like battling that stubborn ketchup stain or tolerating your boss from hell, it was all for you. Your pad, your ride, your belly. Everything spun around you like you were the center of your own universe.

But spoiler alert: Once you're a dad, there's this ticking clock glued to your soul. From that moment till your last breath, it's not just about you anymore. It's about this tiny, screaming, pooping bundle of joy that's half you, half her, and entirely new. You're no longer the lone star in your galaxy; you're part of a constellation now, a duo, a trio, a team. It's the ultimate game-changer. Welcome to fatherhood, dude. It's the wildest ride of your life, and guess what? There's no getting off.

So how do you find comfort in this and not feel like you need an escape?

For a lot of us, the whole "welcome to fatherhood" spiel feels like life's throwing us a pop quiz we didn't study for. A quiz you can walk away from and say, "Fuck it, I don't wanna do this." I ain't gonna sugarcoat it—I flunked that test at first. But I kept at it, scribbling answers, crossing them out, until one day it clicked. I passed. Not with flying colors, but hey, a pass is a pass.

What I mean by that is that if you don't cut yourself some slack for morphing from "just me" to "me and them," you're gonna be on a one-way trip to Regretsville. Without that self-forgiveness, you'll find yourself itching to hit the eject button, craving the good ol' days when it was just you, your whims, and your carefree chaos. It's like giving a pacifier to the scared little kid inside you. But hear this loud and clear: There's a massive difference between being a man with a young heart and a boy playing dress-up in a man's world. Read that again.

Becoming a dad? It's like an extreme makeover for your soul. Almost everything about you will evolve, and it damn well should. Imagine jetting off to a foreign country, a place with weird customs, unfamiliar faces, and a language that sounds like gibberish. At first, you're a fish out of water. But then, slowly, you start soaking in the culture, picking up phrases, changing bits of yourself. Before you know it, you're not the same person who stepped off that plane. You're someone new, someone who's adapted, grown, and heck, even flourished in this strange new land. I know a thing or two about this since not only am I a fucking badass dad of two but I also moved my entire life from Canada to Mexico. *Hola, amigo!*

That's what fatherhood is—a journey to a new you. So don't beat yourself up for not being the guy you were pre-kid. You haven't just changed; you've evolved, blossomed into something even more awesome. It's a freakin' metamorphosis, and it's beautiful, man. You now have the real freedom, the freedom to start over.

Finding peace with this new version of yourself, forgiving yourself for letting go of the old you, it's like opening a door to a whole new world of joy. You get to redefine happiness, redraw the boundaries of freedom. It's a fresh start, a clean slate. And let me tell you, that sense of peace, that freedom to be the new you, it's worth its weight in gold.

By giving yourself that golden ticket of forgiveness, you're paving a brand spanking new path to joy in this "Me & Them" world. It's like opening your eyes for the first time and realizing, damn, you're a dad now. And not just any dad—you're a gem, a dadass, a priceless piece of the puzzle. Gone are the days when you were just a boy, trying to elbow your way through life. Now, you're a man on a mission. A guardian, a guide, a rock. Fuck, that's so beautiful I'm almost tearing up writing this.

Every ounce of effort you pour into them, it boomerangs back at you, but transformed. It comes back as this pure, unfiltered love. The kind that doesn't give a rat's ass about your flaws, past screw-ups, and all those demons you used to have. It's love that loves you for who you are—battle scars, old addictions, and all. This dad gig, it's not just a role; it's a ticket to a life of loving and being loved in a way that's raw, real, and unapologetic.

This life, the dad life, it's like being handed the keys to a kingdom where you get to mold a human life with your values, your beliefs. You've got the freedom to love like there's no tomorrow, to wear your heart on your sleeve, to tear down those walls you've been hiding behind. Your kids, they don't want a dad who's a mystery, locked up in some emotional fortress. They want you, all of you, flaws, fears, and all. You're now fully fucking free to be you, the real you.

And here's the beautiful part: You start finding magic in the mundane, the everyday. Because now, you know your worth. You savor being you, without having to be more, and everything you do for yourself feels like a sweet taste of freedom, but with purpose, with meaning.

Sure, this shift doesn't happen overnight. When I first stepped into the dad shoes, I stumbled. Hell, I face-planted a few fucking times. Fatherhood is like running a marathon with your heart without ever training for it—it's tough, it's relentless, and it's not for the faint-hearted. Being a lousy dad? That's easy. Being a dad who gives a damn? That's where the real challenge lies. Fatherhood is only hard for dads who give a shit.

So take that time, dive deep into your soul. You still have time; it's not too late. Learn to forgive yourself for the sudden growth spurt life threw at you. Embrace your worth, tip your hat to your victories, big and small. And when you do, you'll find that freedom isn't just a concept; it's a living, breathing part of your everyday life. You're not just surviving fatherhood; you're thriving in it.

Such deep fucking stuff, isn't it?

It was hard for me because I didn't have any pals who were in the same boat, no dad-bros to shoot the shit with about diaper disasters and sleepless nights. No one to fucking bro-hug me and tell me that everything was going to be all right. I was winging it, big-time. There were moments, man, so many moments, when I just wished for some seasoned father figure to slap me on the back and say, "Chill, dude, you're doing fine." That's why I'm spilling my guts in this book. To be that guy for you, to assure you that, despite the chaos, the storm does calm down. Eventually. To not freak out and look for the next exit.

Because, holy hell, those first few months? It's like living in a perpetual state of "WTF." Thought watching a Thai ladyboy put a whole Coke bottle up his ass was the pinnacle of crazy? Buckle up, buttercup. Fatherhood's first year is like that, but on steroids and with less sleep. Diapers exploding like grenades, screams that make a banshee sound like a choir boy, and the constant, crippling fear that you're screwing it all up.

But here's the thing: you survive. You adapt. You grow some serious dad-balls. And that's what I'm gonna lay down for you—the raw, uncut truth of how I navigated through the shitstorm of new fatherhood. It's messy, it's gritty, and it's real. But damn, it's the most epic journey you'll ever embark on. So let's dive into the madness, headfirst, with no apologies. This next chapter is all about that madness. It's kind of a horror story in a sense. Enjoy it (but not before bed or you might have nightmares).

Welcome to the club, Papa.

CHAPTER 5:

GO CRAZY OR DIE TRYING

So here I am, using this chapter's title to drop another 50 Cent reference like they're hot, which is kinda hilarious considering my 50 knowledge is limited to, like, five tracks max. The last time I really jammed to one of his beats was back in the stone age of primary school. I remember burning "Many Men" onto a CD that mixed rap, emo, and metal, the kind you crafted like a damn art project using Limewire. Yeah, freaking Limewire & Kaaza. What's actually hilarious is that I'm penning this in 2023. Some of you new dads or soon-to-be dads reading this might never have experienced the sacred ritual of CD burning. If you're like five years younger than me or more, forget it. Hell, you might be scratching your heads, wondering what the hell I'm rambling about.

Burning CDs, man, it was an odyssey. Every step was a brush with danger, a dance with digital devils. You'd fire up your PC (or Mac if your parents had money), only to be bombarded with those government ads plastered everywhere, screaming "Piracy is theft!" They slapped that warning on every damn VHS and DVD and probably in fortune cookies too. Those ads were straight out of an FBI flick, with eagles and badges, threatening to throw your twelve-year-old ass in the slammer alongside hardened criminals, all for swiping a few tunes. Like, seriously? Locking up kids for not shelling out cash at a store for a CD? Absurd.

But did that stop us? Hell nah. We were digital rebels, bro. We'd dive into the sketchy, virus-laden depths of Limewire or Kazaa, crossing our fingers that our family computer wouldn't implode and earn us a week of solitary confinement in our rooms, courtesy of Dad's wrath. And then, there was the second act of this techno-drama: CDBurner. That software was the holy grail. Safe, speedy, and crucial to our mission.

Downloading those tracks was like defusing a bomb—one wrong click, and boom, your computer's toast. But when it worked, man, it was like striking gold.

I'm sure you don't give two shits about this but whatever, dude, it's my book. Here's how it worked.

After an agonizing thirty-minute digital eternity, you'd finally get those softwares up and running… as you blocked the phone line using the internet. The real fun began when you started hunting down tunes on Limewire. If you were after a chart-topper, like "All the Small Things" by Blink182 (back when pop punk was on top of charts), it was a piece of cake. A quick search, a clean download, and boom—you got yourself a pristine mp3 file, ready to be immortalized on CD.

But oh boy, if you were chasing something less mainstream, you were about to embark on a digital safari through the Wild Wild West of the internet. You'd click on what you thought was a rare punk track, only to be ambushed by an audio clip from some unholy midget porn. Or maybe you'd stumble upon the audio version of "2 Girls 1 Cup"—by then, it was practically a rite of passage; everyone had seen it, heard it, talked about it. It was like the messed-up national anthem of the internet.

And let's not forget those downloads that turned out to be some questionable Taliban executions. You'd sit there, headphones on, wondering if you just accidentally tuned into some top-secret terrorist radio. Or you might get lucky and just end up with a dude accidentally recording his jar-breaking rectal nightmare. Again, that video was pop culture back then. Real classy stuff.

But the worst? The absolute worst was when you'd finally think you snagged that obscure track, only to discover it was a godawful recording made on a cassette player in some dude's Honda Civic. You could practically smell the fast food as he ordered a McFlurry with nuggets and Big Mac sauce at a McDonald's drive-thru in Alabama. The whole transaction, including the sound of him fumbling with change, became an unintentional part of your music collection.

Once you finally, miraculously assembled your playlist, the real magic happened in CDBurner. You'd wrestle with the CD tray, cursed by your brother's grape juice fiasco, and finally get that blank disc in. Hitting "Burn" was like launching a space shuttle. You'd then embark on a marathon wait, praying to the tech gods for no errors.

By the time you started this whole circus at 10 a.m., took a lunch break while your downloads crawled along (one of which turned out to be granny porn, for Christ's sake), and finished your list around 2 p.m., you'd be hitting that "Burn" button at 2:30. Fingers crossed, you'd hope to have that musical masterpiece ready by 4 p.m., just in time to show off at your grandparents' house over the weekend. And if all went well, your Discman would be blasting those hard-won tracks, each one a battle scar from your journey through the digital trenches. Ah, the glory days of internet piracy—a mix of adventure, horror, and a dash of accidental porn. God, I miss the 2000s.

Quickly after, MP3 players came on the market, shit became easy, and life got slowly more and more depressing.

Now I'm about to start writing about the period of my life as a dad that I thought I'd never recover from, or maybe just kill myself in the process, while listening to any music I want to with zero downloads needed and not even a fraction of a second of loading play time on my phone directly in my Bluetooth headphones. And just for the sake of making this random ass intro make sense, I'm putting on "In da Club" by 50 Cent right…now.

Saying the early days of parenting is tough is like saying getting kicked in the nuts is "uncomfortable." It's a fucking understatement. I've hammered this point home earlier in the book, but it bears repeating: fatherhood is a bitch, but only for the guys actually giving a damn. If you don't see your role as a dad or future dad as important, then it'll be an easy deal for you. Sure, some dads might read this, smugly boasting about their angelic little girls who snooze like logs and coo like doves at feeding time. But for the rest of us mortals? It's not just hard; it's a descent into the seventh circle of hell. All my friends with daughters had it somewhat rough, but I have two boys…. I lived hell (and still do sometimes).

If you think I'm spewing hyperbole, think again. There were nights I'd have gladly taken a gut punch from Mike Tyson, hoping to hurl up my guts—and maybe rediscover that coin I swallowed in fifth grade as a dare in exchange for a blueberry muffin—rather than face another midnight wake-up call from my own personal banshee. Every damn night, it's the same horror show. Your eyes are practically glued shut, and when you finally pry them open Clockwork Orange style, the world's a blurry mess because, of course, your glasses are MIA in the pitch dark. And God forbid you flick on a light—that's like signing your death warrant, because your baby mama transforms into a she-werewolf, ready to rip your head off for disturbing her precious three minutes of sleep.

You can't blame her for being cranky in the middle of the night. My wife is a fucking warrior who had two C-sections. Imagine the aftermath of that barbaric surgery. They sliced her open like a horror movie extra, shuffled her organs around like a deck of cards, then zipped her up with staples like she's some sort of human Ziploc bag. Postpartum, her hormones were more whacked out than a vegan chowing down on Bill Gates' lab-grown, Play-Doh-looking, chemical burger monstrosities, dreaming of the real meat they wish they could have.

So you end up standing in that dark kitchen, waiting for the goddamn bottle warmer to heat up the milk, which feels longer than watching the extended cut of *Lord of the Rings*. Meanwhile, my kid (who in this moment doesn't feel cute anymore but more like Gollum) is screaming his lungs out, probably waking the cranky upstairs neighbor—the same one who's had it out for me ever since I mistakenly used her trash bin for a load of stinky diapers.

Writing this is like reliving a war. It's PTSD-inducing, no joke. But through all that hell, those sleep-deprived, sanity-testing nights, you learn something about yourself. You learn you're tougher than you thought, that you can love more deeply than you ever imagined, and that maybe, just maybe, this whole dad thing is the wildest, most messed up adventure you'll ever love being a part of. But fuck, why do we not get proper training for this shit?

Let's get one thing straight: prenatal classes? They're about as useful for real parenting as a chocolate teapot. You learned how to change a diaper? Congrats. A blind monkey could do it. You might think you're all set, armed to the teeth with parenting books, Google-fu, and all the war stories your folks could muster. But here's the gut punch no one tells you about: the mental mindfuck that comes with a newborn. It's like being thrown into the deep end of a pool filled with Jell-O—you can't swim, can't float, just flail.

I'm writing this book for a reason. This is the real shit, no filter.

Every one of us is wired differently, with unique triggers and breaking points we didn't even know existed. "What are triggers?" you might ask yourself right now while reading this in your undies in bed. Emotional triggers, bro. They're like those sneaky landmines in your brain's backyard. Picture this: You're just strolling through your day, cool as a cucumber, when bam! Some random thing—a song, a smell, hell, even a look from someone—goes off like a firecracker in your head. Next thing you know, you're feeling all sorts of crazy, like a pinball machine of emotions. It could be anything from a blissful memory of your first kiss to that time you got pantsed in high school gym class.

These triggers are like spiritual Post-it notes from the universe, reminding you of stuff you've got packed away in the attic of your soul. They're not just there to mess with your mojo; they're a cosmic nudge, a way for the universe to say, "Hey, dude, remember this feeling? Time to deal with it." That's why doing your inner work as a new dad is crucial... it's time to deal with this shit before you take it out on your family.

Before kids, the biggest stress might've been a flat tire or a bad Tinder date. But kids? They're like tiny, adorable terrorists, expertly crafted to push buttons you didn't even know you had.

It's a crossroads, buddy. You've got two choices. You can either let these moments of insanity sculpt you into a more badass version of yourself—a parenting ninja, a wiser human being because you've put the time and effort into doing your inner work—or you can crumble like a stale cookie at the mere sound of a baby's wail.

And let me assure you, these kids, they're relentless. They test your limits in ways that would make even a Zen master lose their shit. We're talking about tests that make *Survivor* look like a walk in the park. Diaper explosions that resemble a scene from a horror movie, tantrums in the cereal aisle that make you wish for a swift alien abduction, and sleepless nights that leave you hallucinating more vividly than a Woodstock attendee.

It's a very sleep-deprived, sanity-questioning, why-the-fuck-did-I-do-this moment. It's like boot camp for the soul. You come out on the other side tougher, wiser, and with a heart so full it could burst.

As a new dad every day is a test, and every test is a story you'll laugh about...eventually. You might cry about it first...like I did.

The first time I got slapped by the cold, clammy hand of parenthood, it felt like my emotions were hijacked by a drunk, blindfolded pilot. I completely lost control of my emotions and it haunted me for a long time after that. We're talking just days after my first son escaped the hospital's clutches. I fucking hate hospitals, man. Those dad chairs in hospital rooms? I swear they're crafted from the finest concrete with the thinnest layer of fake leather you've ever seen, designed to flatten your ass like a pancake at a highway diner. My poor ass was sore for days after that hospital stay. And the dread? Palpable. Strapping my kid into the car seat was like prepping a bomb for transport—one wrong move and boom, tears and poop everywhere.

Gone were the days of the magic nurse button, summoning a caffeine-fueled, Croc-rocking nurse who'd seen it all. She'd breeze in, smelling of stale coffee and existential despair, somehow convincing us that our son's latest alien noise was "totally normal." Bitch, please…can you just comfort me? And those doctors, doing their rounds like they're ticking off a grocery list: Baby? Check. Mom? Check. Dad? Ha, as if they give a rat's ass. Let's be real, once you're in the dad zone at the hospital, you're about as visible as a fart in a hurricane. It might not be everyone's experience but it was mine, both times, and it sucked hard.

Having a baby in a hospital is like trying to perform a high-wire act while juggling flaming swords—thrilling, but you're glad there's a safety net. My wife and I, we were like the dynamic duo of hospital births. Both our boys popped out in the sterile embrace of a hospital, even though my wife, the ever-brave soul, wanted to play home-birth roulette with our second. But, hey, she's got this rare blood thing that's more temperamental than a cat on a hot tin roof, so hospital it was—a place where blood bags are as plentiful as bad cafeteria coffee. Also since she already had an emergency C-Section for our first son, she had to go the same route for the second one.

Let me tell you, though, hospital births, man, they're like this bizarre blend of a sci-fi movie and a poorly planned vacation. You're cocooned in this bubble of false comfort, so disconnected from the raw, gritty reality of life that it's almost laughable. And the thing is, when we finally got discharged,

I was strutting out of there like I was the king of fatherhood. But then, the first wail from my kid in our apartment hit me like a ton of bricks. It was like discovering that your favorite bar has been replaced by a vegan smoothie shop—utterly disorienting and a bit frustrating.

Everything I thought I knew about my kid and being a dad in general was tossed out the window. His cries were like a foreign language, his stares seemed to question my very existence, and his feeding schedule? More erratic than all of Justin Trudeau's promises. All I could think was, what in the actual fuck is happening? Am I even cut out for this dad gig? It's like one minute you're playing life on beginner mode, and the next, it's switched to expert without any warning. If I couldn't do Guitar Hero, how the fuck am I going to be able to do Daddy Hero? Trust me, I hate hospitals, but for a very short moment, all I wanted was to be back there with all the help.

Now that I'm a bit older and wiser (though, let's be real, a good wet pussy fart still gets me every time), I've had some time to chew on what went down when my son first came home. It was fucking ugly and it's all my fault. And I've come to realize, it wasn't just normal; it was as predictable as a hangover after a night of tequila shots and Colombian whites.

Think about it for a second: As an adult, just moving from one apartment to another is like trying to solve a Rubik's Cube blindfolded. Stress city. And for my generation? We're so weak most of us lose sleep over it for weeks pre-move. Or that first night in a hotel room on vacation, tossing and turning like a salad in a blender. We've seen some shit in our lives, but a change of scenery still throws us for a loop. It's about the vibes, man. It's just facts. Every room, every space has its own energy, and that shit gets cranked up to eleven when you're hopping from one place to another.

So, picture my baby boy, fresh out of the womb. He's gone from the cozy, muffled world of my wife's belly to the sterile, beeping chaos of a depressing hospital, and then—bam—in the blink of an eye he's in a Montreal apartment, complete with a blinged-out golden bidet (Italian owners), curtains that look like a fruit salad barfed on them, and a garbage disposal that sounds like a monster truck rally. The kid's world has been flipped, turned upside down, more than the Fresh Prince.

And there I was, a twenty-three-year-old rookie in the dad league, clueless as a penguin in a desert. His crying was like a siren in my brain, and I couldn't soothe him for shit. I felt like he was rejecting my touch, and it was messing with my head. *Does he not love me anymore?* I was snapping at my wife, feeling the walls closing in, and seriously contemplating whether a double vodka soda at 9 a.m. was a bad life choice. It was five o'clock somewhere. I was crumbling, dude. Like a cookie in a toddler's fist. I felt like the poster boy for *Loser Dad Magazine*.

So, just then I remembered a diamond nugget of advice from a client of mine, a dadass veteran with four kids, and two of them being twins. He said, "When you're about to lose your shit as a father, just step out for a sec. Cool off. You'll make more damage in the room than leaving your kid alone in that same room." Because, let's face it, shaking a baby? That's not just a no-no, it's the kind of horror show that keeps you up at night. You can cause serious damage, even death. And hell, you don't bring a kid into this world to go all Hulk on them. But I'm no fucking idiot so that never crossed my mind, and I hope with all my heart it will never cross yours as well.

I was teetering on the edge, man. So, I did just that. Gently laid my son in his crib, bolted to the bathroom, and plopped my ass on the cold ceramic floor. He was in his crib, his room. He was safe. Nothing could happen, because the menace was me. I kept telling myself: I'm fucking Oliver Kult, not some drywall-punching Kyle. But the urge to let loose was clawing at me like Wolverine fresh out of the lab. Good thing I didn't have a Monster energy drink that morning or the wall was meeting Mr. Right Fist.

I was sitting there, sweating buckets, heart pounding like a Joey Jordison (RIP) drum solo, jaw clenched so tight I could crack a walnut. It was a full-blown meltdown. Britney '07 type of shit. A couple of minutes later, I dragged myself back to my son's room, scooped him up, and just lost it.

Tears streaming, snot bubbling, and out popped this pathetic, sobbing "sorry" from my lips. I was pissed at myself for letting it all spiral out of control. I'd loved this kid since I was nineteen, dreaming of being a dad, and there I was, unraveling at the sound of his cries.

This was day three of his life, and we hadn't even hit the real scary stuff. We were still queuing up for the roller coaster that is parenthood. Looking back, I kick myself for not working on my own shit sooner. The moment I knew I was going to be a dad, I should've been on a mission to iron out my flaws. No more rage as my go-to emotion; no more raising my voice to win points in an argument.

I'm a dad now. And I want to be a badass one, not a bad one. It's time to level up, to be the man my kid needs me to be. Turning every freaky emotion into anger? That's not just weak; it's the definition of pathetic. I need to be stronger, not just for me, but for him, for our bond. We as dads need to be stronger. It's about transforming into the dad that's not just there, but fully present, emotionally solid. A dad who can weather the storm without turning into a human tornado.

Reflecting on those early months with my firstborn, let me tell you, the list of regrets is longer than a family of five's Costco receipt. How I acted, how I felt, the vibes I threw at my kid—if I could hit rewind, I'd do it in a heartbeat. Sure, I've leveled up to badass dad status now, and in my kids' eyes, I'm the best damn father this side of the galaxy. But if I stumbled upon some sketchy Mexican pawn shop selling a time-travel remote like in *Click*, I'd be all over that thing. Would I give up an arm and a leg? Maybe not literally—hobbling around for the rest of my dad career doesn't sound too hot. But would I guzzle down the sweat of a reality TV star from *My 600 Pound Life* for a shot at a do-over? Hell, sign me up. If Steev-o did it in *Jackass*, I can too.

The truth is, I'm not the only dad who's screwed the pooch a time or two or more. Every dad out there has bungled it up somehow. Different strokes for different folks—we've all got our own triggers, our own baggage, our own shit we need to work on.

And if you're sitting there thinking, "Not me, I'm Father of the Year. I regret no moments because I was always perfect," well, buddy, you might want to check your ego at the door and take a long, hard look in the mirror.

But hey, maybe you're a dad-to-be, and this chapter's got your anxiety going like a Red Bull-fueled hamster on a wheel. Don't sweat it. The fact that you picked up this book, that you're soaking up my tales and tribulations, that's a step in the right direction. It means you're open to learning, to getting better, to not repeating the same dumbass mistakes I did. Or at least, now, you know you're not alone sometimes drowning in guilt.

This book, I hope, ends up not just a bunch of words on paper. To me, it's a toolbox, a survival guide for the dad jungle. Hopefully, it'll help you sidestep some landmines, or at least recognize when you've stepped in it and know how to scrape that shit off your boot faster and smarter. So keep reading with your ego aside. Because we can all learn something from another dad.

One thing you won't be able to run away from is the hectic sleep schedule. The sleep deprivation game is real, and it's a total mindfuck. Look, any health guru will tell you, an average Joe needs like 8-10 hours of solid Zs to function at his peak. That's not bro science; it's legit—hit up Google if you think I'm bullshitting. All these "motivational" dudes on Instagram and TikTok saying they thrive on five hours or less of sleep are full-blown liars. Eight is the bare minimum to remain sane.

Even before the little diaper fillers crash the party, tons of guys are already screwing themselves over. I mean, they're up until the witching hour, eyes glued to TikTok, watching some halfwits scarf down Tide pods or fake-twerking to the latest Drake track. Or they're swiping right on filtered-to-hell-and-back chicks with OnlyFans who'd probably charge you extra to watch paint dry.

These dudes are burning the midnight oil, then dragging ass to the gym at dawn, trying to build a physique that isn't sustainable, thinking they're doing themselves a favor. Spoiler alert: They're not. They're just pre-gaming for the dad-life sleep-deprivation marathon. But this isn't a thing where "practice makes perfect;" you can't get good at being tired.

And let me tell you, when you do enter the dad zone, it's like reliving those wild teenage years when you popped a speed pill in the back of a rusty Honda Civic, minus the fun, the Four Look, and the cheap cigs chain-smoking. Remember how you felt crashing after a night of partying, rolling that last Kush blunt, trying to mellow out, only to crash for a day and a half and still wake up feeling like a zombie straight out of *The Walking Dead*? That's fatherhood in the early days…months. But you never get that marathon sleep. It's like running on empty, nonstop.

And don't even think about compensating with nuclear-grade pre-workouts. That stuff's basically one molecule away from meth. Sure, it'll keep you buzzed, heart racing as fast as Jacques Villeneuve, but it's like putting a Band-Aid on a bullet wound. You're just setting yourself up for a heart attack or some mutant cancer, all while still being a cranky mess who can't regulate simple emotions.

The reason so many dads end up snapping at their kids isn't some complex psychological puzzle. It's plain and simple—they're fucking exhausted. Running on fumes, trying to keep it together while their brain's screaming for a timeout. It's a brutal cycle, and it takes a toll.

In so many cases, dads are now the only ones working during the day while baby mama is on maternity leave at home with the baby. As a freshly minted dad, it for sure feels like you've been through a fucking intense emotional warzone. You've got the adrenaline highs of rushing to the hospital, the mind-boggling spectacle of childbirth where you're seeing things you can't unsee (like your girl dropping a "rabbit poop" and her female parts stretching like some kind of magic trick), and then the euphoric moment of meeting your kid and realizing your life's changed forever. It's a roller coaster of emotions, from pure love to pants-shitting fear of screwing up as a dad. And just when you're neck-deep in this new reality, bam, you're back at work like you just had a regular weekend. With everyone expecting you to act fucking normal.

Your boss thinks two days off is a generous paternity leave. Why not, right? He's a baby boomer, and that generation of men used to go right back to work a few hours after birth like a bunch of heartless, beat-up dads. So, you're back at the grind, running on fumes, trying to keep your head above water. Trying to keep your brain focused on what you need to do. You're juggling the pressures of work and home—and sleep? Ha, that's a long-lost friend. You're so damn tired, you start acting like a stranger to yourself. It's like you're watching some B-movie of your life where you're the weird main character. You can't even parallel park anymore. What the fuck is wrong with you. right?

Listen up, dude. You need rest. And I'm not talking about cracking a beer, flopping on the couch, and zoning out to the game while the baby's napping. That's not rest; that's just a timeout. Real rest means when that little bundle of joy hits the hay, you do too. Nap time for baby, nap time for daddy. S-L-E-E-P.

And if you're lying there, eyes wide open, mind racing while the baby's out cold, then it's time to rethink your game plan. It's not about numbing yourself with booze or zoning out in front of the TV. It's about healing, recharging, getting your body and mind back in the game. You've got to find a way to rest up properly because running on empty isn't just bad for you; it's bad for the whole goddamn dad show.

I was still a kid myself in a lot of ways when I first got thrown into the dad ring. Looking back now, I was still an immature prick. So, when my firstborn started doing the every-two-hour wakeup routine, my wife and I hashed out a plan. She hit the bed at 9 p.m., and I was on night duty till 3 a.m. Then I'd crash till 8 or 9. Sounds like a plan, right? I was getting close to six hours of sleep overnight and I just had the schedule of a bartender. I thought I was smart— so I stocked up on vodka for homemade cocktails, parked the crib next to the couch, and spent my nights grinding out *Tony Hawk's Underground*, thinking I was the king of multitasking.

There I was, doing kickflips in Russia and slamming triple vodka sodas, while my little guy was waking up for feeds. I'd mix another drink while the milk was warming up, feed him, give him a big kiss and get him right back to sleep, and dive back into doing tricks in front of a strip club in Tampa. See the fucking problem? I wasn't really resting when he slept. My brain was on full-throttle, wired from the game and booze. Was it calming my nerves down? Felt like it, but it wasn't really.

The whole sleep shift thing with my wife wasn't a half-bad idea, but man, looking back, I could've played it so much smarter. Instead of zoning out on Xbox and booze, I should've been giving my body some real downtime. Meditation, breathwork—stuff that sounds like hippie bullshit to disconnected Matrix people but actually works wonders. That would've made a world of difference in those first few months of zombie mode.

But hey, I was somewhat of a dumbass—didn't know any better back then.

You have to realize that meditation isn't just for those bald, Zen-like dudes chilling on mountaintops wearing kimonos. It's for every Tom, Dick, and Harry out there—especially for the sleep-deprived, over-stressed dads. You don't need to levitate or chant in Sanskrit. What you do need is the guts to stop running from your feelings, to quit numbing yourself with whatever your poison is, and just sit your fat ass down, close your eyes, and feel. That's it. Simple, but not easy for most.

Meditating is easier than changing a damn tire in the pouring rain on a busy highway, so don't give me that "I can't do it" crap. There's no excuse not to try it, especially when you're desperate for some semblance of rest to be the best version of yourself. If you want to grow, you have to give yourself the tools to do so.

You might think this spiritual stuff is a bunch of hooey, but hold up—it's not just about beliefs; there's real, hardcore science backing this up. When you close your eyes and focus on your breath, feeling the air flow in and out of your nostrils, some magic starts happening in your brain. It begins to release chemicals, the good kind, that balance your hormones.

Feeling like you're on edge because you're not sure if you fed your kid the right amount of baby mush? Meditate. Your brain will start to lower your cortisol levels, dialing back the stress. Feeling a bit down in the dumps because your life's been nothing but diapers and drool since you became a dad? Meditate. Your brain will boost your serotonin, lifting your spirits without needing a drop of booze or a hit of whatever.

And if your mood's all over the place because of crappy sleep? Meditate. Your brain will kick up your natural melatonin production, so when you finally hit the sack, you'll dive into a way fucking deeper, more restorative sleep faster than you can say "night-night."

It's like giving your brain a much-needed tune-up. You're not just sitting there with your eyes closed; you're actively participating in your own well-being. You're tuning in to your body, giving it what it needs to reset, recharge, and kick ass as a dad.

It's a harsh truth, and it's fucking sad, but most of us guys, we're not wired to chill out naturally. We've been fed this macho BS that real men grind nonstop, that taking a break is a sign of weakness, something only pussies do. But, let me tell you, that's a load of crap. It's a one-way ticket to Burnout City, population: you and all the other unconscious dads.

Take a hard look at yourself the next time you lose your cool. You're flipping out because the TV won't turn on and your kid's screaming for Cocomelon like it's the end of the world. You're whacking the TV, cursing under your breath—but hold up. Stop. Ask yourself, "Am I tired?" Nine times out of ten, the answer's going to be a big, fat yes.

It's not about denying you're tired or stressed; it's about recognizing it and dealing with it in a healthy way. If the idea of meditation seems like some hippie-dippie stuff to you, think again. It's about giving your mind and body a break, a chance to reset.

Breathwork, just like meditation, is also a big-time game-changer. There are so many techniques out there that you can learn easily, each targeting different parts of your body and mind. When you tune in within yourself and listen to what your body's screaming for, applying the right breathwork technique can be a total lifesaver. It's like giving your system a much-needed reboot. You'll find yourself more rested, more in control of your emotions, and ready to face the dad challenges head-on.

Neither meditation nor breathwork eats up your time. You don't need a Zen garden or a mountaintop. Hell, you can do it on the shitter if that's the only peace you get. I'm laying it straight—I only started bringing meditation and breathwork into my life in recent years. If I'd started sooner, I probably wouldn't have lost my cool so much with my kids. And trust me, it shows in their behavior now. They're like little mirrors, reflecting back my own reactions to frustration and anger from when they were tiny. Now, I even do Breathwork sessions with my kids. Imagine that, they are four and seven years old, already learning to regulate their emotions through breathing. It's such a powerful tool and it's amazing to watch.

But you know what? Before learning about all that, I ended up in couples therapy, spilling my guts about being a dad and a husband. And to be honest, it was one of the best things I ever did. That therapist helped me take a step back, understand my reactions, and tune into what my body and mind needed. Let me tell you, there's no shame in asking for help. Doing so isn't just good for you; it's good for your kids too.

The last thing you want as a dad is to be seen as weak, because weak men, they don't evolve. They break under pressure, or they just keep spinning their wheels, never learning, never changing. But not you. You're not weak. You're here, you're ready to grow, to be that hero for your kids.

Realize this: Everything in fatherhood starts with you—the good, the bad, the ugly. The sooner you acknowledge that, the sooner you can start doing the work. It's about becoming the dad you know you can be, the one your kids will look up to, the one they'll brag about to their friends.

Meditation, breathwork, therapy—these aren't signs of weakness; they're tools of strength. They're your secret weapons in the wild world of fatherhood, especially in those early months of this crazy roller coaster. Embrace them, use them, and watch how they transform not just your life, but the lives of those little humans who depend on you.

CHAPTER 6:

DO AS I SAY, NOT AS I DO

The first time my kid dropped an F-bomb, it was like a very funny yet horrifying milestone. Picture this: He's barely out of diapers, still wears them at night because even the most intense urges to drop the biggest shit of his life doesn't seem to wake him up, and already spewing out "fuck" with a giant smile on his face like he's auditioning for a Tarantino movie role. I'm not exactly a poster child for etiquette, so it wasn't a huge shocker that it came early for the little man. But, thank the stars, it wasn't his second word after "dada." That would've been a tough one to explain at the next family Christmas dinner, right?

Now, being a Quebecois transplant, my vocabulary's a colorful mix of English and French

swear words. Esti, Caliss, Tabarnack, Criss—
these are the spices of my daily language, like if
Gordon Ramsay hosted a Quebecois version of
Hell's Kitchen. And here's my kid, soaking it all
up like a sponge. English is my second language,
picked up from my *RuneScape* days—yes, major
geek alert—so my accent's as mixed as a thrift
store record collection.

I had to sit the little guy down and explain that
words like "fuck" and "shit', and their French cousins,
are adult words. Heavy stuff, not for kids. It's like
giving a toddler a chainsaw—hilarious in theory, but
a disaster waiting to happen. Landon, bless his heart,
got the message. He nodded seriously, like a mini
professor, but I could see the mischief in his eyes.
He was planning his next linguistic adventure, and
I could only hope it was not during a PTA meeting.

So there I was, having this epiphany, right? Like
a bolt from the blue, it hit me—kids are like those
annoying mime artists, except they're cute and you
can't just walk away. They mimic everything. The way
you strut around the house like a B-list celebrity, the

way you mumble "what the fuck" under your breath when you step on a Lego, even that weird eyebrow thing you do when you're confused—it's like they've got a built-in copy machine. Good or bad, they'll fucking pick up on it fast and copy it in no time.

And it's not just the small stuff. Oh no. They'll pick up your accent, your expressions, the whole shebang. You say "son of a bitch" when you drop a spoon? Congrats, now you've got a mini-me swearing at cutlery at every meal. It's like having a tiny, judgmental mirror following you around, reflecting all your quirks and foibles. Some of this stuff sticks like gum on a hot sidewalk. You'll see them doing something and think, *Damn, that's all me*. Other things, they'll drop faster than a hot potato as they grow up. Stressful? That's putting it mildly. It's like someone handed me the world's most important manual and said, "Good luck, buddy. No pressure." I knew being a dad I had to behave better but that early in my child's life? 24/7? Fuck me.

Every step, every word, every facial twitch is potentially a lesson for this tiny human. It's enough to make you want to walk around wrapped in bubble wrap, speaking in polite whispers. But who am I kidding? I'm as subtle as a sledgehammer at a glassware convention.

It makes you realize how much of a mess you sometimes are. It's like the universe is throwing you this existential pop quiz: Am I going to be the "ah, fuck it, it is what it is" dad or the "let's get my shit together" dad? Guess what? Option two is the only way to fly. But man, it's like trying to teach a cat to do yoga—sounds good on paper, but it's a whole different beast in practice. They've done it with goats, though…but that's another story.

Realizing that your everyday habits—the cursing, the half-assed manners, the "it's five o'clock somewhere" attitude—might not be the golden standard is like a slap across the face with a wet fish. It stings, it smells, and it leaves a mark. And it's not just a tiny "oops" moment. It's a full-blown "what the hell have I been doing all these fucking years" crisis.

There's this theory that's both horrifying and enlightening. It's like a horror movie that's so good you can't look away.

It's like a psychological and spiritual gut punch. It says that when someone else—let's say your kid, your partner, or that guy who always takes the last donut at donut day at work—pisses you off, it's not just about them being annoying. It's like holding up a mirror to your own messed-up insides. We're talking deep, dark, "I don't want to go there" territory.

In psychology it's called "projection." It's like your brain is playing hot potato with your issues. Instead of owning up to your own crap—like maybe you're a control freak or have the patience of a toddler on espresso—you slap those traits onto someone else. "It's not me, it's you," right? Classic move.

But wait, it gets better. Or worse, depending on how you look at it. In spiritual circles, they say the outside world is just a big, fat reflection of your inner circus. So, if your kid throws a tantrum and it sets you off like a firecracker, maybe it's because deep down, you're also a bit of a hothead. It's like the universe is handing you a "Know Thyself" quiz, and buddy, it's an open-book test.

Now, as a new dad, this stuff hits harder than a hangover after a bachelor party. You start to realize, every time little Landon's antics make you want to pull your hair out, it's not just about teaching him to behave. It's about figuring out your own triggers. Why does this bother me? What's it saying about my own issues?

The thing is, as much as it feels like a kick in the teeth, it's actually a golden ticket to growth. You don't just want to be a dad; you want to be a damn great one, right? That means facing the music, doing the hard work, and coming out stronger on the other side.

As men, we're a little like late bloomers in the self-improvement garden compared to women. We either stroll through life in blissful denial of all the work we have to do on ourselves or we're too chicken to admit we're a fixer-upper. No problem buying a 1967 house that barely stands to fix it and flip it, but fixing us within? Fuck no.

But then comes fatherhood and that's a hell of a wake-up call.

Back in my younger days, my fatherhood dream was like a sitcom highlight reel. I'm talking about teaching the kiddos soccer, globetrotting family vacations, Disneyland, mini-golf, trampoline parks, and ice cream at the park—all that picture-perfect, Instagram-worthy stuff. I wanted to be the dad I felt like I never had. My old man? He signed me up for soccer but never kicked a ball with me. He'd watch every game but dude, why not play with me?

Then playtime with toys or video games? Forget it. So, there I was thinking, *I'll be different. I'll be the cool dad.* And all I'll have to do is do all these things I always wished my dad did with me.

But fuck, being a dad isn't just about being the king of playdates or the master of vacations. It's about being the best version of yourself. Figuring out what needs to change deep inside of you and do the work to change it. See, my dad, he did what he knew without any significant growth, but I've realized there's more to this gig. It's not just about what you do with your kids; it's about who you are around them and around others.

The real MVP move in fatherhood? It's healing yourself early into this big adventure. Working through your baggage, your triggers, your flaws. Why? Because your kids are like mini detectives; they pick up on everything. If you're a ticking time bomb of unresolved issues, guess what? You're not just dad; you're a walking, talking lesson in how not to handle life.

All that fun stuff—the soccer, the trips, the ice cream—that's great, it's important, but it's the icing on the cake. The cake? That's you, pal. A dad who's worked through his shit, who understands himself, who can be there for his kids in ways that go beyond just playing catch.

That's the dad they'll remember, the dad they'll thank and the dad they'll want to be later (if you got boys like I do).

Everything else? It's just sprinkles on the sundae.

After having this awakening, I started to work on my personal issues and fast. Because not only is my kid now copying everything I do and say, he sees me as a fucking hero. And I'm not the type of guy to take that role easily.

Now, to be fair, my kids are not the first person to see me as their hero. Let's rewind to a time when another person saw me as their hero—a moment steeped in the kind of class you can only find in a back alley dive bar.

Long story short, one of my exes, a girl with the kind of enthusiasm for oral work that would put most pornstars to shame, once decided to give me the sloppiest blowjob I've ever had the pleasure to receive right in the middle of her parents' kitchen. I'm talking a mouthful of saliva the equivalent of a cast of *My 600 Pound Life* entering McDonald's. This "reward" was offered to me after I MacGyvered a bottle of wine open using a picture frame screw because, let's face it, who needs a corkscrew when you've got a drunk barber's ingenuity?

The backstory? She was all tangled up in some teenage-level drama with her childhood friend— the kind of spat that's about as interesting to me as watching paint dry. She's distracted at her job, nearly gets canned, and suddenly, I'm looking down the barrel of funding her beauty routine. There's no way

I'm going to be the one paying for those pink fake nails. They do look good on my junk, but I can't afford this shit. She'd racked up more warnings at work than I had questionable life choices. And yeah, okay, I might've been responsible for a couple of those—showing up late to drop her off because my time management skills are as polished as a muddy boot.

But back to the kitchen heroics. When I unscrewed that $12 bottle of vino, using nothing but a screw from the wall and her dad's trusty screwdriver, I might as well have been wearing a cape. In her eyes, I was the Paw Patrol, the Avengers, and the Justice League rolled into one. It's a funny thing, the way a booze-soaked brain turns a simple act into a heroic feat. It's like finding a diamond in a mountain of coal—doesn't happen often, but when it does, boy, do you feel like the king of the world.

Another time someone called me a hero was over ten years ago. Remy, my old buddy from the wild days of my stoner youth, had a night with me that's gone down in the annals of "That was fucking Epic" lore. We were seventeen, brash, and as smart as a box of rocks. A beat-up car, a Walmart parking lot at the witching hour, and us two geniuses hotboxing it with the worst fucking weed known to man, so bad it'd make a skunk gag. Remy's car, an old rusty Honda Civic with a subwoofer so big the trunk would barely close properly, decided to play dead because we, in our infinite wisdom, left it running for nearly two hours while we turned the inside into a Cheech and Chong tribute.

Now, Remy's dad, a real entrepreneur, was enjoying a state-sponsored vacation (read: jail) for trying to smuggle kilos of that terrible weed across borders in his very bright orange Hyundai Santa Fe. Before his extended stay at the gray-bar hotel, he had told Remy about some extra "herbal supplements" hidden at their family cottage. The mission for his son was clear: bring the weed to a certain "Patrick" so he could afford to buy packs of smokes inside jail walls. Being the dutiful son, he moved the goods but made sure to keep a pillow-sized stash for personal use, our personal use. We smoked that botanical garbage like it was going out of style.

My brain, swimming in a sea of Blue Cool Gatorade and THC, hatched an epic plan so insane it just might work. My bladder was about to burst from all the Blue Cool I'd guzzled down, and there was Remy's gasless car, sitting there like a challenge. 1+1 = 2 right? So, what does any self-respecting, highly baked hero do? I unleashed the fat hose in the frigid Canadian February air and gave his car a golden shower some perverted girls out there would dream of right in the gas tank.

Did it work? Hell yes. Did it mess up his engine? Like a tornado in a trailer park. And if you're curious about how long it takes to get the stench of stale gasoline off your cock, the answer is two excruciatingly long days despite washing it twice a day with Irish Spring soap bars. But in the grand tapestry of our teenage stupidity, that night was a masterpiece. To this day, when Remy gets a few too many under his belt, he'll recount the tale of how I saved the night with nothing but a full bladder and questionable decision-making skills. In his booze-soaked brain, I'm not just a hero; I'm a freakin' legend.

All of these stories and more in which I'm the fucking hero are more often than not filled with booze and poor decisions. The feeling of being a hero in those times does not compare in the slightest bit to when I am one to my kids. To say that being a hero does feel amazing, not just when the payout is leading to you busting a nut or sticking it in your wife's butthole or becoming a legend to a lowlife thirty-year-old drunk truck driver, but it's more about feeling like you have a massive impact for someone you care about. Having kids allows you to get that amazing feeling almost daily.

So here I am now, Super Dad, minus the cape and spandex. To my kids, I'm like a cross between a tattooed Thor and a handyman. Squashing unwanted spiders in their bedrooms? Check. Retrieving their favorite Spiderman toy from the deep end of the pool? Done. I'm the go-to guy for all their pint-sized crises. It's an ego trip, sure—every dad secretly digs being their kid's first hero.

But then, my brain starts doing cartwheels. What happens when my little dude heads to school and starts looking up to other people? That thought's like a cold shower on my superhero parade.

Flashback to my school days, and I'm this awkward kid, treating the older students like they're rockstars. I was so low on self-esteem, I would've believed anything they said. "Dye your pubes pink to be cool?" Sure, where's the hair dye? It's like I was auditioning for a role in the *Desperate to Fit In* sitcom.

But was it my fault for being so gullible? Hell no. As a dad now, I get it. If your old man doesn't help you build some solid self-love, you're gonna end up thinking the grass is greener everywhere else. And let me tell you, that's a one-way ticket to Anxietyville, with layovers in Depression Central.

I'm now thirty years old, covered in tattoos, got the whole badass look going on, with a family that's like something out of a glossy magazine. And yet, there are days when I'm questioning if I'm half as cool as the next guy. Lack of confidence? It's like a silent alarm—you don't have to say it; it just rings.

And guess what? My oldest son Landon, he's a chip off the old block—struggling with the same self-confidence game. It's like watching a mini replay of my own life. It's not just about squashing spiders or rescuing toys anymore. It's about teaching him to squash doubts and rescue his own confidence. I want him to break the cycle.

Fatherhood's more than just the heroics and high-fives. It's about passing on the real stuff—self-worth, confidence, the power to believe in himself. It's about breaking the cycle, laying down new tracks. I'm not just raising a kid; I'm trying to elevate a future man, one who won't have to dye his pubes pink to feel cool. That's the real superhero gig—no costume needed.

So, here's the million-dollar question: How the hell do you break these goddamn cycles? I mean, the last thing I want is for my kids to start idolizing some half-assed posers, thinking they're the second coming of the Beatles, and then spiraling down some loser vortex. This whole mess starts and ends with me. Well it started with my own fucking parents, but let's not go there—this isn't a therapy session.

For real, though, I gotta pump up my self-esteem like it's a deflated football at the Super Bowl. Sounds easy, right? But let me tell you, for a guy who's spent three decades marinating in "I'm not good enough" sauce, it's like trying to climb Everest in flip-flops.

But hey, I'm not one to back down from a challenge. No way, Jose. Anything's possible when you fucking want it hard enough for yourself and for your kids. So, first things first, I'm flipping the script. Instead of trying to sprinkle my day with bullshit positivity that feels as fake as a three-dollar bill until I can mindfuck myself into believing I'm the shit, I'm putting a full stop on the self-trash talk. Here's what I mean: Let's say I hang a picture frame, wifey says, "Wow, looks great," and my usual line is, "Eh, it's kind of crooked because I suck at this shit, but yeah, it's not that bad." It's like I'm the king of self-deprecation.

The problem is that every time I drop one of these self-dissing bombs, it's like I'm giving my kids the green light to beat themselves up too. Just like daddy does, because they want to be like daddy. It's like teaching them that self-doubt is some sort of family tradition. "Oh, Dad's shitting on himself again; must be a Tuesday." That's not the legacy I want to leave. I'm better than this.

So, I'm slamming the brakes on that crap. No more "I suck at this" or "I'm just not good enough." It's about showing my kids that it's cool to be proud of what you do, even if it's as simple as hanging a damn picture straight. They need to see their old man owning his stuff, not just with words but with attitude.

But wait, there's more to this self-rescue mission. I gotta start strutting around like I own the place, not like I'm renting space in my own life. It's time to walk the walk, talk the talk, and maybe throw in a little swagger for good measure. It's about setting the stage where self-respect is the headliner, not the opening act.

That's step one. Now, step two.

I gotta stop tossing in the towel like a chump every time things get rough. Lately, I've been the undisputed champion of the "ahh, fuck this shit" league. And let's be real—that's pretty damn pathetic. If I'm aiming to raise my kids to be stand-up humans, brimming with confidence, they need to see that life's a tough gig, but we don't just fold like a cheap tent. Because when you start folding it over and over again, it always ends up breaking.

The fact that you're flipping through this book— my book, written from my own damn hands—is a testament to me kicking my give-up habit to the curb. A step in the right direction. Yeah, I wrote this whole shebang, a whole tree's worth of paper, spilling my guts about the wild ride of fatherhood. Going on and on about how amazing this journey is to me as much as it is terrifying. And let me tell you, it's been a love-hate relationship with every damn word written. There were times I wanted to slam the delete button so hard it'd need therapy. I had to keep reminding myself that this book isn't for me; it's for all the other dads out there, and for their kids. So here we are. I've fucking done it.

I'm betting my right hand on this idea: If I show my kids that their old man is no quitter, no little bitch-ass loser, they'll take the hint. Monkey see, monkey do (monkey pee all over you). It's about setting a bar so high that they'll be vaulting over my accomplishments before they're even out of high school. Because daddy was always a quitter even as a kid.

I want them to see their dad grinding it out, pushing through the bullshit, coming out the other side with a grin. It's not just about finishing what you start; it's about showing them that when life throws a haymaker, you don't hit the canvas—you swing back, harder.

If I can pull this off, if I can be that never-say-die, tough-as-nails role model, my kids are gonna soar. They'll tackle life with a grit and determination that'll make my struggles look like child's play (not the movie). That's the goal, the dream, the plan. No more Mr. "Ah, Fuck This." It's time to be Mr. "Bring It On." Bring on the challenges, the hardships, the uphill battles.

It used to be "Do as I say, not as I do," but I want to be proud to say "Do as I do" and watch them live their best fucking life.

But for this badass, never-give-up attitude to really take root—for me, for you, for every dad out there—we've got to be all in. Present. Engaged. It's about putting in the blood, sweat, and tears, and making damn sure our kids see it. But the system, society, the whole damn machine is rigged against us. It's like trying to swim upstream with a backpack full of bricks. They don't want us around our kids.

Now, I'm about to spill the beans on why I hightailed it to Mexico and why I've got this burning, fiery hate for the godforsaken system in North America. It's like a giant, soul-sucking vacuum, designed to keep dads like us on the sidelines.

We're supposed to be the breadwinners, right? Clock in, clock out, bring home the bacon. But while we're slaving away, life's passing us by—our kids' lives, our family time, the moments that actually mean something.

Anyways, ready to read a pissed-off chapter?

Middle fingers up. Turn the page.

CHAPTER 7:

F*CK THE SYSTEM

Here's the raw, unvarnished truth I gotta lug around in my memory for eternity, unless some voodoo hypnotist can zap it outta my brain: My dad's sporting a forest of pubes like it's going out of style. No joke; we're talking a dense, untamed jungle, like he's harboring a goddamn wildlife sanctuary down there. It's like stumbling upon a lost Amazonian civilization every time you catch a glimpse.

You can't unsee that. It's seared into my brain, like a traumatic tattoo.

But thank the stars for that overgrown, untamed pubic hedge. It's like a natural-born privacy screen from the universe, blocking the full Monty from traumatizing my young, innocent eight-year-old eyes.

It's like a bizarre, twisted stroke of luck. It's like having a censor bar that's made by Mother Nature. If it wasn't for that, I'd have an unwanted, permanent mental image of my dad's junk burned into my memory. A prospect more horrifying than a *Friday the 13th* movie marathon.

Another thing I know about my dad is that he's been rolling with a denture since he hit the sweet sixteen. Yeah, you heard it. Picture this: Every night, the dude has to pop out his chompers like he's disassembling a damn Lego set before crashing into bed. Now, fast-forward to a time when he's having oral sex for the first time. Going down on a girl for the first time is already a bit stressful, but imagine his challenge with fucking dentures. The scene's set, he's about to dive into the deep end of ladyland, and his brain's firing off like a machine gun at a carnival shoot with a bunch of questions.

First up, he's nosediving downtown and bam! He's hit with this fish market whiff. He's thinking, "Is this the norm? Did the sex-ed teacher skip the chapter on Eau de Vagina?" Then, he's in the thick of it, all systems go, and he's wrestling with strategy. "Do I go full merry-go-round with the tongue action or stick to the tried and true vertical tango? Fast? Slow? What's the winning combo here?"

But wait, it gets better. The ultimate curveball—his denture. Yeah, that's right. Amidst all this, his brain has to be screaming, "For the love of all things holy, don't let my fake teeth stage a freakin' mutiny mid-act." What a nightmare.

Here's the batshit crazy truth about my old man's chompers. It's not like he snagged a set of dentures after a fistfight with a goddamn gorilla in the Amazon during a wilderness safari. Nah, the dude simply had teeth more twisted than Jeffrey Epstein's morals, and braces? Forget about it, too rich for my grandfolks' blood. So, they opted for the bargain bin solution: dentures, cheaper than a happy hour special.

And get this, my dad's an accountant. Yeah, thrill-a-minute, right? But hold onto your hats, because this bean counter once dated a chick with her own freaking indoor pool. I stumbled on this info when I was renting a place with one, and he just dropped it into conversation like it was no big deal. I was burning with questions. Who was this mystery woman? When did this steamy romance go down? How the hell did she have enough dough for a pool playground? And the million-dollar question: Did he bang her in those chlorinated waters? Is he the kind of man who likes wet sex?

All I really know about my dad is he's glued to the TV, soaking up news and hockey like a sponge. That's my dad for you, a walking, talking enigma with a set of false teeth and a past shrouded in mystery and indoor pool sexcapades. That's pretty much all I know about him.

Living in my dad's pad for the better part of eighteen years—yeah, I did the whole angsty, emo cave-dweller routine for a couple of those, headphones glued to my ears pumping The Used, Fall Out Boy, and My Chemical Romance—but still, you'd think I'd have the old man figured out. But nope, I could probably scribble everything I know about him on the back of a Taking Back Sunday concert ticket. It's nuts when you think about it.

I used to chalk it up to the times, like maybe dads from his vintage just came off the assembly line programmed to be snooze-fests, locked up tighter than Fort Knox when it came to personal stuff. But then, at this one double dinner date my wife and I had with her friend and this guy (the guy's not with the chick anymore, and his name's slipped my mind like a fart in a tornado), I got this eye-opener. This dude was regaling us with stories of his acid-tripping parents, taking him on these wild boat odysseys, spilling their guts about everything under the sun— love, dreams, the whole enchilada. Pure, unfiltered heart-to-hearts out on the open sea. The guy was still super close with his parents, despite him living in Mexico and them kicking back in good ol' Cali. They had a connection that made my rapport with my parents look like two strangers nodding at each other in an elevator.

This got the wheels in my head spinning like a DJ at a rave. So I did some research and I dove headfirst into the world of the '70s, trying to decode these hippie parents. It's like trying to make sense of a Salvador Dali painting at first. Some of these flower children were raising their kids in a utopian, no-rules lovefest, while others were as uptight as a pair of jeans in the dryer set on "shrink to fit." It's all about keeping up appearances, climbing the social ladder. I grew up thinking this was the way to go, but as I'm getting older the idea of it makes me sick.

Because the truth is, it all comes down to how much you're willing to sell your soul to a sick society, to Big Pharma, the big, bad system. It's like, are you gonna march to the beat of society's drum, or are you gonna crank up your own playlist and dance like nobody's watching? That's the secret sauce in the parenting stew, regardless of the era. You're either in line with the status quo or you're out there painting your own, wild, Technicolor dream. And comparing that with my own gig as a dad? Man, it's like comparing a rock concert to a library reading for kids. Total eye-opener.

Around the age of sixteen, maybe seventeen, on a typical, godforsaken hangover Saturday, I was dumping a measly fifteen bucks of gas into my '98 pale blue Toyota Tercel—a real beater, but damn, those things are indestructible tanks. I've had more than one in my time; actually owned three of them), and I swear, if it wasn't for my wife's intervention, I'd still be rocking one, cruising around like some low-budget Mad Max.

I shuffled into the gas station, ready to snag my daily dose of adrenaline—a sugar-free Monster. Yeah, to this day, I've quit the smokes, ditched the drugs, even turned my back on all types of porn, but energy drinks? Those cans of sweet, sweet nectar are my Achilles' heel. It's like trying to kick a habit that's superglued to your hand. I keep telling myself I'll quit before I turn thirty-five…still got four years to go.

I was standing in line at Couche-Tard, and right in front of me was a lady who looked like she'd been marinating in Pepsi and microwavable slop for the past decade. She was probably forty-five but looked like she'd been dragged through her fifties backward. Next to her was her daughter, about my age, but man, she was as vanilla as they come. Total "girl next door," while I was over there with my tastes firmly planted in the emo/goth camp—you know, the kind of girls who look like they could summon bats with a snap of their fingers. That was my shit.

I'd bet my last dollar I'd never seen this chick at my school. She had that vibe of someone who'd be at home in some uptight all-girls Catholic joint while I was slumming it in a public high school that looked more like Alcatraz than an educational institution. I'm actually the only child in my family that went all five years of high school in that horrible school. Punishment from my parents for being a jerk child? I'll never know. But me and that girl, we were like two different species—she a pedigree poodle, and me a pit bull that had been kicked one too many times.

For the sake of the story, let's call the mom "Karen." Karen gave me this look, her face twisting up like she had just caught a whiff of week-old roadkill. It was the kind of look that could curdle milk. Her daughter, let's dub her Little Miss Priss, spun around, and man, she was not even trying to be discreet. She was gawking at me like I was a freak show exhibit, her eyes wide like saucers, probably wondering if I was gonna sprout horns and a tail right there in the gas station.

Karen leaned in, whispering to Little Miss Priss like she was sharing state secrets. But with her voice raspier than sandpaper from what I could only guess was a passionate love affair with those Benson & Hedges, she was broadcasting to the whole damn store. "You better never bring a punk like that back into my house," she hissed, like I'm the boogeyman come to life. Little Miss Priss, doing her best impression of a bobblehead, shook her head so hard that I was half expecting it to pop off and roll down the aisle.

At this point I was left with two ways to react.

I could tap Karen on the shoulder and, with the biggest, cheesiest grin plastered on my face, tell her, "Yo, lady, even if the fate of the world hung in the balance, I wouldn't go near your daughter. She's got about as much appeal as a wet sock, and looks like she'd give head like a horse munching on corn—all teeth, no finesse."

Or, I could just zip it, play the part of the oblivious punk, let them think they were whispering under the radar. But nah, that wasn't my style back then. That's what thirty-year-old Ole would do because I ain't going to waste my energy on negativity. But sixteen-year-old me was a savage. I was all about making a statement, so I went for the gold—option three.

As Karen was there, swiping her fancy Visa Platinum, acting like she was the queen of the gas station, I unleashed the beast. I'm talking a fart so loud, so foul, it was like a declaration of war. This thing had a presence, a personality. It echoed through the gas station like a clap of thunder, turning heads, parting the Red Sea of customers.

I swear, you could almost see the green cloud of it, a Monster energy-drink fueled toxic miasma that would make a skunk blush. Karen's face? It was a picture worth a thousand words—a mix of shock, disgust, and a hint of begrudging respect. Little Miss Priss looked like she was about to faint, her pristine, sheltered world rocked by the raw power of my gastrointestinal prowess.

That was my mic drop moment. Sure, I was decked out in my wolf tee, ink crawling up my arms, looking every bit the troublemaker Karen pegged me for. But if she was going to dish it out, she'd better be ready to take it. Ain't no high-and-mighty, judgmental Karen gonna throw shade my way without getting a taste of her own medicine.

There's not a damn moral to be found in that gas station showdown. It's like a *Seinfeld* episode—a story about nothing that's somehow about fucking everything. In this chapter, though, we're diving into the deep end. It's all about how the system, that big, faceless machine, shoves dads into this neat little box, slapping a "Do Not Disturb" sign on their Dadass potential.

If you're thumbing through these pages, snug as a bug in your system-programmed cocoon, you're probably thinking, "This guy's off his stupid mind. A regular punk-ass, an anarchist, probably thinks his brainwaves are being intercepted by alien frequencies." And you know what? I've heard it all before. Call me a tinfoil hat wearer who believe aliens are as real as my left nut. Say I'm the type to scream, "The moon landing was a soundstage production!" from the rooftops. I've been tagged and bagged with every label in the book since forever (just like at the gas station; I told you this story connected somehow).

This chapter isn't some conspiracy theory manifesto. I'm not about to lead you down a rabbit hole lined with Illuminati symbols and subliminal messages in Disney movies. Nah, this is about cracking open your skull—metaphorically, calm down—and pouring in a fresh perspective. It's about looking at the society we've been cookie-cutted into and asking, "Is this really it? Is this the best we can do, or can we be better dads?"

We've been molded, shaped, and sculpted by a system that loves nothing more than a good old status quo. It's comfortable, it's predictable, it's as exciting as watching paint dry. But here's the thing: It doesn't have to be this way. We can be more than just cogs in a machine, more than just cookie-cutter dads living cookie-cutter lives.

Who knows, you might even discover your own version of Dadassery hiding under that well-groomed, system-approved exterior. Or you might just decide I'm full of it and put down this book forever. Either way, it's going to be one hell of a chapter.

Let's kick this off with a fact that's as spine-chilling as bumping into Michael Jackson in his latter years down a pitch-black alley. That kind of heart-stopping, "Am I in a horror movie?" moment. We're talking about something that sends shivers down your spine, makes the hairs on the back of your neck stand up like you've just mainlined a double shot of espresso straight into your fear glands.

In America, the average parent spends less time with their kids than a conspiracy theorist spends on YouTube. We're talking less than two hours a day. Let's put this into a perspective that even my ex-goldfish can understand (I'm saying "ex" because like every goldfish ever bought by a human it ended up in the toilet after we left on vacation and asked my neighbor to feed it..and he never did).

Now, surveys—those things we all fill out when we're avoiding real work or to get some random, useless reward from a suspicious-looking-blog type website—reveal that the average adult takes about twelve minutes for a standard poop session. And no, we're not talking about the "after Taco Tuesday" kind of emergency; we're sticking to regular, run-of-the-mill poops here. Sit, take the phone out, scroll, push, wipe, and move on.

So, let's crunch some numbers, shall we? With adults reportedly visiting the porcelain throne twice a day (because one poop is never enough (if you're a healthy dude), plus a few bonus rounds to drain the lizard, we're clocking in roughly 30-35 minutes daily in our personal bathroom sanctuaries. That's about 25 percent more time than we spend with our kids. Imagine that! We're more committed to our bowel movements than our bloodline. It's like if we decided to up our bathroom game to four times a day, we might as well move our mail there, but it still wouldn't take up our whole day.

Yet, for some mind-boggling reason, most of us are totally fine with this parental time allotment. And let's be clear, when I say "time spent with kids," I'm not talking about quality time like staring into their eyes as they recount their day while daydreaming about having a fat burger for dinner. No, sir. For some, "time spent" includes chauffeuring the little ones to soccer practice while mentally replaying last night's game or plopping them in the tub and then zoning out to TikTok while they're in there making a shampoo mohawk or the classic "look, Dad, I'm Santa" soap beard.

This isn't quality time; it's more like being an unpaid Uber driver and a lifeguard rolled into one. Shouldn't we, as parents, strive to spend at least two solid hours a day actually engaged with our kids, doing stuff together that doesn't involve a screen or a steering wheel?

Now, before you think I'm just here to shamelessly parent-shame, hold up. I'm not dumping all the blame on parents. Most of us could definitely up our game, but let's be real—the system is as much to blame. It's like being in a three-legged race with a kangaroo—it sounds fun until you realize you're both trying to hop in different directions. We're navigating a world that doesn't always make it easy to balance the books of life, let alone find quality time for the little humans we're responsible for. So maybe, just maybe, it's time for a rethink on how we prioritize our days, even if it means a little less time in our ceramic thinking pods.

This minimal time spent with our kids begins quite fucking early in their lives.

In my "in the system" dad life, it started with my oldest kid's first day at daycare. I was whipping out my phone like some paparazzi dad to snap a pic of Landon. There he stood, this little dude in his shark backpack with his name embroidered on it, rocking Spiderman velcro shoes that I was secretly green with envy over, and a classic smiley face Nirvana tee that his mom picked out (Mom's a Cobain fan). The kid looked so damn cute it was almost criminal.

But a bunch of shit was happening inside my head—I was wrestling with how to feel about this whole scene. On one hand, should I, like a dominant Gorilla, be puffing out my chest, proud as hell that he's stepping out into the world, showing off his independence like he's some mini-CEO of Toddler Inc.? Or, should I be kicking myself, feeling like a grade-A loser dad for handing over my flesh and blood to a bunch of strangers with septum piercings and infinity tattoos?

Yeah, I get it. It's important for him to mingle with other little minions his age, learn the ropes from someone who actually knows what they're doing (I'm hoping). But on the flip side, isn't it a bit messed up that he's spending more time with some daycare guru than with his own father?

So, why's everyone acting like this is the norm? Like we're all just supposed to fall in line and hand over our kids before they're even done teething? We held off sending Landon to daycare until he hit the big one-year mark, scoping out every joint in town like we were on some top-secret mission. But get this—on his first day, I found out he was practically an old man there. They had a whole crew of babies, some barely old enough to hold up their own heads.

It just feels off, you know? Like we're missing a crucial part of the parenting manual. I'm trying not to judge; really, I am. But I'm throwing shade left and right like Simon Cowell at a bad *American Idol* audition. Seeing these tiny tots, barely out of the

womb, getting dropped off at the crack of dawn—
it's like, what the hell are we doing? Where did we
take this wrong turn into Crazytown? Don't mothers
want to still hold their precious babies tight? Don't
fathers want to protect their bloodline at all cost?

It's like society's got this twisted evil script we're all
blindly following because we've been indoctrinated
to prioritize work and money, ditching our parental
duties before the ink on the birth certificate is dry.

Choosing a daycare for your kid is like playing
Russian roulette with a very powerful Nerf gun—
you're hoping for the best but bracing for a face full
of way-too-hard foam darts. You stroll into these
daycares, and they're all sunshine and rainbows, the
owners grinning like they're selling timeshares in
heaven. They're slinging this pitch like every toddler
who crosses their threshold is on the fast track to
being the next Mark frickin' Zuckerberg or some
mini Dalai Lama of modern times.

What you're really scoping out is if the shitters are
clean (knowing that's where most kids spend time at
with their billion diaper changes) but not like "creepy

uncle with a van" clean, you know? You're checking for those little plastic outlet covers so your kid doesn't go full-on E.T. finger and end up sizzling like a McNugget. And the grub—you're praying they're not just shoveling sugar and processed crap into these kids like they're prepping for winter hibernation.

So there I was, a half awakened/conscious dad, having a full-on existential crisis. Was sending my kid to daycare at twelve months like throwing him into the lion's den with a steak strapped to his back? Was I rushing this?

But let's be real, I gotta work. It's not like I can whip up a skin fade and textured top while juggling a wiggly, twenty-pound toddler. And I'm pretty sure my barber homies wouldn't appreciate a shop soundtrack switch from Gucci Mane feat. Lil Baby to a non-stop CocoMelon and Paw Patrol remix feat. Baby shark.

Turns out, the daycare we picked wasn't the ninth circle of hell. They actually got the kids outside, even in the urban jungle. They had a green park very close, fed them better than my sixteen-year-old self living off Subway steak and cheese footlongs, and had them doing arts and crafts that didn't look like a glitter bomb went off.

Landon even started making pals, some of whom I'd let into my house; others I wouldn't trust with a barge pole. He was digging the daily routine, and slowly I was shedding that dad guilt like a snake skin. But there's this part of me, the dad I am now, that wishes I'd listened to that gut feeling. Maybe I should've worked out a way to keep him home longer, soak up those baby years a bit more. It's like looking back at your high school yearbook—equal parts nostalgia and "What the fuck was I thinking?"

Makes me think of family gatherings. You know those family Christmas parties, right? The ones with drunk cousins who can't hold their liquor, chain-smoking aunts rocking the '80s hairstyles puffing like chimneys, creepy uncles who give off that "don't let a woman leave her drink unattended around him" vibe, and grandparents who look like they've been taxidermied a few years ago? Then, in the middle of this festive freak show, your kid decides it's showtime. Suddenly, he's Picasso with a plate of mashed potatoes, splattering the walls, yelling like a caveman ready to fight a grizzly bear, throwing a tantrum on the floor like you've just punted him with steel-toed boots after he asked you to put on *Bob the Builder* on TV.

And amidst this delightful chaos you try to run away from every year with a different excuse, your least favorite relative, who's probably had one too many eggnogs and forgot to put on deodorant, slurs out that cliché, "Enjoy these moments, bro. It goes by so fast." Yeah, right. Like I haven't heard that one a million times. This is usually the sentence people tell you when you're running on fumes from seven weeks of sleep deprivation, your sex life's as exciting as a seventy-three-year-old's bingo night, and your kid's channeling his inner demon.

Every time some well-meaning but clueless relative dropped that line, I'd snort and think, *Can't wait for this hellion to grow up*. But, writing this book, man, it's like a slap in the face at those face slap competitions. I was wrong. It does fly by, and hell, I do miss some of it (not the potato-painting episodes, though; I hate cleaning up).

Lately, I've matured a lot and been doing a lot of meditation and breathwork, trying to level up my soul and my dad game. And I keep getting these flashbacks. Sometimes in the form of legit flashbacks but sometimes in the form of messages from the universe. Like, what if I'd only sent the kids to daycare a couple of days a week? Kept them with me some days, with my wife on others, and then the whole clan together on weekends? What if I had changed my schedule to ensure my kids spent enough time at daycare to familiarize themselves with being around other hellraisers but still spent the majority of their days with us?

These thoughts keep doing laps in my head. Every time I'm sitting there, trying to find my inner Zen master, I'm haunted by these "what-ifs." And that's okay. That's exactly where the inner work starts. It's like this gnawing question chewing on my brain: Is this what good parenting looks like or did I fuck up? Just outsourcing your kid and calling it a day? Or is the real MVP move being there, hands-on, 24/7? Or is that too fucking much?

Oh, but wait, it gets better. Daycare's just the appetizer in this Chinese-type cheap unhealthy buffet of system-sponsored dad-neutering. The main course? Your kids' health. And they start this shit young with the whole vaccine circus. Every six months, like clockwork, they're herding you in, telling you to roll up our kid's sleeves for shots against diseases that haven't offed anyone since the days people were riding horses to work and sexting was done on paper and sent by pigeons. It's like they're jabbing not just our kids, but our opinions and instincts right in the ass.

And that's what it's like for the whole medical merry-go-round in America. As a dad who gives a damn, who's trying to do right by his kids, it feels like you're just another cog in this giant, faceless machine. Your gut feelings? Tossed out the window. Your questions? Drowned out by the sound of prescription pads flapping in the breeze so Mister Doctor can get another free yacht party with Brazilian models sponsored by pillmakers.

It's like, "Hey, don't worry your pretty little head about it. Just trust us—we're the professionals." Yeah, professionals funded by Big Pharma, with their pockets as deep as the Grand Canyon. They've got us by the balls, man. "Don't question, don't think, just follow the herd." It's like they've got this playbook, and if you so much as think about calling an audible, you're treated like you've lost your fucking mind.

It's like the education and medical systems in this so-called land of the "free" have a vendetta against dads. It's as if they're plotting in some shadowy back room, scheming up ways to keep kids as far from their fathers as possible. What's the endgame here? Are they trying to churn out a generation of daddy-issue-ridden robots? I think so.

Look at the stats—the cold, hard facts. When Daddy's MIA, the kid's more likely to keep that absentee father tradition alive. It's a gift that keeps on giving, just like herpes. It's like passing down a family heirloom, except it's a crappy one. And it's also true when you look at the impact of growing up without a solid male role model. We're talking lower voting rates, fewer caps and gowns at graduations from high school all the way to university, and slim chances of landing those cushy, high-paying gigs. This isn't me yanking this out of thin air—it's straight out of the *Annual Review of Sociology* and a truckload of other studies you can read all by yourself if you wish to be as shocked as me. Don't believe me? Go ahead, hit up Google. It's all there, black on white.

Now, I'm not a dumbass; I connect the dots. What happens when you raise a kid without a strong father figure? You're practically manufacturing a society of pushovers, ripe for the picking. These kids are like clay, ready to be molded by whoever's pulling the strings. And who's benefiting? The fat cats, the one-percenters, the guys with their names on skyscrapers. They're up there, getting fatter off the system while the rest of us are scraping by.

It's like we're living in a factory farm for human beings. The system's feeding us just enough to keep us alive, but not enough to think for ourselves. They're banking on us dads being too tired, too busy at work, too damn beaten down to question anything. It's a cycle, a well-oiled machine cranking out generation after generation of people who are too worn out to fight back.

But guess what? I'm not buying what they're selling. When I look at what generations of my family looked like before me and where I was headed myself, I fucking know this has to end with me and my kids. I'm breaking the mold, one dad moment at a time. It's time to wake up, smell the bullshit, and start rewriting the script. They want a society of drones? Well, they're not getting it from my house. I'm raising thinkers, doers, and questioners—not just another cog in their evil machine.

When faced with all these soul-sucking guidelines of society living in this cookie-cutter suburb in St-Bruno, Quebec, it came to us. And it's like, "Wait a minute, what the hell are we doing? We can just fucking move." We're just another set of drones in the hive, feeding our kids to the system, watching them get churned out like factory products.

It's a goddamn wake-up call. We're looking at our kids, thinking, "Do we really want them to turn into suburban zombies? Sitting in those soul-sucking classrooms, lined up like little prisoners, staring at walls with no windows, breathing recycled air, drinking fluoride-filled water, and getting a measly hour of outdoor "freedom" a day?" Hell no. Not my fucking kids.

So, what do we do? We flip the script. We're not about to play the part of the complacent, suburban parents, nodding along while the system fucks us in the ass as deep as Adriana Chechik has been. We decide it's time to bail, to get the hell out of Dodge.

We sell our house, the one we snagged right before Skyler came into the picture. Pre-pandemic. It's a tough pill to swallow, leaving behind a place teeming with memories, where every nook and cranny tells a story. But it's a sacrifice we're willing to make.

Next thing you know, we're packing up our lives and hightailing it to the jungles of Mexico. That's right, the freaking jungle. We're trading in our snow shovels for machetes. We're going off the grid, out of the box, into the wild. Our new backyard? It's not manicured lawns and white picket fences; it's Mother Nature in all her untamed glory.

We want our kids cut from a different cloth, not stitched into the same old pattern. We want them awake, alive, and in tune with the world, not just existing in some suburban bubble. The white picket fence dream family I envisioned and dreamt of since I was nineteen is no more. Now, I want a jungle tribe.

Moving to Mexico, man, that was the most "out of character" thing I have done in my entire adult life. I mean, I ditched the music touring gig—a wild ride of drugs, sleeping in a beat-up '94 Ford Econoline that had more warning lights than a Christmas tree—to become a barber. Why? Because barbering was my golden ticket to stability, something as rare in the touring world as a sober roadie who didn't steal merchandise from the band.

I had this whole plan mapped out: open up my own barbershop, settle down, buy a house, have a commute shorter than a beer run, cozy up with the neighbors, and live out that picket fence dream—you know, kids running around the front yard, a golden retriever named Toby or Max, the whole nine yards. But then 2020 hit, and my wife and I, we looked at each other and said, "Fuck it. Let's toss that stability out the window." Balls to the wall, we got this.

So, we booked it to Tulum, Mexico. I had my Spanish skills from fifth and sixth grade, so yeah, I could count to ten, ask to hit the bathroom, and order a beer—I was practically a local, right? But when we landed in Tulum, I quickly realized, it was a bit like Gringoland. And let me tell you, most of these expats couldn't care less about blending in. They were walking around like they owned the place, not bothering with even the basics of Spanish. It was cringeworthy, like watching a toddler throw a tantrum in a five-star restaurant.

This overprivileged attitude of American and Canadian expats, it was like a slap in the face to the locals. We swooped in with our wallets fat, buying condos, flipping them into Airbnbs, while the folks who'd lived there forever were getting by on Coca-

Cola, beans, and rice. It's like we were playing Monopoly but they were stuck with the boot piece every damn time and always ended up in jail.

But us? We were not about that life. We were here to mesh with the culture, not steamroll over it. I was not about to start chugging Coke and growing a handlebar mustache, but I was damn sure gonna learn Spanish like I was not fresh off the plane. I wanted to speak it without sounding like a bumbling tourist. We came there to embrace the freedom it had to offer and the open mind this country had toward education. I was in no place to teach them jack shit.

It has been three wild years since we uprooted and planted ourselves in Mexico, and let me tell you, I haven't looked back once. The number one question I get, hands down, is about safety. "Aren't you scared for your kids?" they ask, eyes wide like I've moved my family into a war zone filled with landmines and machine guns screwed on top of cars.

I can't help but laugh. Sure, Mexico's got its share of cartel craziness. It's no secret, and it sure as hell ain't pretty. Corruption? Yeah, it's like a national sport down here. But you know what? It's all out in the open. No hiding it. It's the bad guys doing bad guy stuff, and sometimes, believe it or not, the regular Joe gets a slice of the pie. The city doesn't approve your construction plans? Give some extra money—*todo bien*! You've been driving with an expired license for years? Give the cop some pesos—*todo bien*!

Now, compare that to Canada. Oh, Canada, with its squeaky-clean image. But let me burst that bubble for you—it's cartel land up there too, just wearing a different mask. The government's playing the same dirty game, only they're doing it in suits and ties, smiling for the cameras while they pick your pocket. Tax this, tax that. It's corruption with a polite "sorry" tacked on the end.

People watch these Hollywood movies about Mexico and think we're dodging bullets every time we step out for a pina colada and a cigar. Like there's a 50/50 chance of some dude walking into the beach club, AK-47 blazing because of some cartel beef. Newsflash: that's not the daily special down here.

Meanwhile, back in the States, what's the real horror show? It's kids walking into schools, locked and loaded, ready to settle scores over some playground beef from years back. That's the real roulette, the kind that makes Mexican cartels look like a Saturday morning cartoon.

So, am I worried about my kids' safety here in Mexico? Hell no. You know why? Because they don't even go to school in the city. They go to a part-time school in the middle of the jungle.

This school we've got our kids in down here in Mexico, it's like a big middle finger to the North American education system. It's the antithesis of that brain-numbing, soul-sucking routine they've got going on up north to brainwash your kids into become slaves to the state.

First off, this place doesn't kick off at the ungodly hour of 7:30 a.m., like they're trying to turn kids into mini Wall Street brokers. You know the drill—shoveling down a quick, sugar-laden cereal breakfast because you have no time to cook them a proper healthy breakfast, wrestling them into uniforms they fucking hate wearing, slinging a backpack full of books heavy enough to give a bodybuilder a run for their money, then hustling them off to the bus stop in the pitch dark like you're dropping them off at boot camp.

No, sir. Our school down here in the jungle starts at 9:00 a.m. Why? Because it lets the whole family ditch that demonic alarm clock. No more stressful mornings. We wake up with the sun like our ancestors did for millennia. It's like living in sync with the planet, not against it. It's this crazy concept where kids—and parents—get to start their day like human beings, not factory workers on the assembly line.

We're talking about a school that actually respects the natural rhythms of the human body. It's like they understand that kids' brains aren't ready to crank out equations and dissect Shakespeare at the crack of dawn. They get that a calm, unhurried morning sets the tone for the entire day. Even if they do wake up sometimes before sunrise, they have the time to play, draw, read, run outside, or do whatever they desire to do before getting down to learning.

It's a game-changer, man. Instead of starting the day with a cortisol-fueled frenzy, we're easing into it all together in a better mood, ready for new teachings.

Another curveball this jungle school in Mexico throws to regular system schools—a big, fat no to any Disney, Marvel, or any of that capitalist, mainstream media jazz on clothes. Now, don't get me wrong, I'm not some anti-fun dad. I still dig watching those Marvel movies with my boys. I'm a big sucker for Doctor Strange and all the multiverse stuff they now have going on. But at this school, the vibe's different. They're not about turning kids into walking billboards for corporate America.

The philosophy's pretty clear: Those hyper-stimulating cartoons and movies? They're dopamine factories, man. They light up a kid's brain like a Christmas tree. So, when you've got a swarm of kids decked out in superhero tees and Elsa dresses, it's like a distraction bomb. Pulls them away from the now; makes it tougher for them to focus and appreciate the simple joys at school.

When I first heard this rule, the last Matrix conditioned bits of my brain were like, "What in the actual fuck? Are we joining a cult of the most boring people on earth?" But then, I saw it in action. Kids in plain, unbranded clothes—it's like a chill pill for the entire school. It's not about squashing their individuality; it's about dialing down the noise, the constant bombardment of "buy this, want that."

The vibe's calmer, more grounded. Kids aren't competing for who's got the flashiest Spider-Man shirt or the sparkliest Frozen backpack. They're just kids, plain and simple. No distractions, no consumerist peacocking. It's a return to basics, to a time when a kid could just be a kid, not a mini consumer-in-training.

The school's curriculum? It's like they took the best parts of Montessori, threw in a dash of Waldorf, and then stirred in a hefty dose of local Mayan culture to pay respect to the land where the school is sitting. The result? A curriculum that's more like a love letter to nature, self-love, well-being, and culture than a lesson plan. Trust me, it doesn't take away from learning. Kids come out of there as sharp as Gordon Ramsey's knives.

Classes aren't just confined to four walls, a chalkboard, and a burned-out concerta-addicted teacher. Nah, they're as likely to be held under the canopy of trees as they are indoors. It's like Mother Nature's the head teacher, and the great outdoors is the classroom. Learning math while sitting on branches; reading science books while swinging in a tire hanging from another branch.

If you're not hip to what Montessori and Waldorf schools are all about, and I don't blame you, the system doesn't promote this stuff at all any fucking where. Do yourself a favor and Google it. It's like finding out school doesn't have to be a soul-sucking experience. Waldorf's all about educating the whole kid—not just stuffing their heads with facts. Making them copy-and-paste robots. They dive deep into a subject, and then wrap it up in creative arts like painting, music, and drama. It's like a buffet for the brain, where every part of a kid's mind gets to feast.

Montessori, on the other hand, is about setting kids free to explore their world. It's not just about learning; it's about respecting life and understanding the forces at play in nature. That's the vibe we're feeling here in this jungle school. It's about giving kids the keys to the world and saying, "Go ahead, explore. Make it yours."

Now, how does this stack up against the education gulag my kids would've been locked up in back in Canada?

Back when I was hitting the books (because that's pretty much all we were doing) in primary school in the '90s, it was nothing like this jungle school paradise. And lucky me, I was part of the guinea pig year for Quebec's brand-spanking-new education reform. You know what that means? Bunch of new shit teachers had no idea how to teach to us so most of it felt like a big "Kids, just read the fucking book and answer the questions." They had spent years before my class came through rewriting this and tweaking that, figuring out new ways to grade us, what kind of mind-numbing homework to dump on us. By this point in the book, you've probably picked up on the fact that I'm not exactly government's number one fan. To me, it's all a pile of bureaucratic BS controlled by big corporations with brown envelopes and extremely deep pockets.

I see these lawmakers and officials as these out-of-touch yahoos living in their ivory towers, clueless about what's really going down in the trenches. Most of them being baby boomers who actually got everything handed to them on a fucking silver platter. They're just stirring the pot, making changes for the sake of keeping their cushy, high-paying gigs, because deep down, they know the system was better off when kids were learning real skills from their dads, hitting the books only if they had some lofty career aspirations beyond that.

Call me old-fashioned, but I wish I grew up in a world like that.

Instead, there I was at seven, same age as my oldest kid now, trudging to this dreary school with about as many windows as a bunker. I spent hours parked on one of those orange plastic chairs with the screechy metal legs, lined up in rows like we were on some assembly line. It was less "nurturing young minds" and more "prepping for a lifetime of cubicle life."

In that school, creativity and curiosity were about as welcome as a wet fart in a fully packed elevator. It was all about falling in line, following the script, and if you dared to color outside the lines? Well, you were in for a world of trouble. You were being put on medication right away because, well, who the fuck wants a kid who thinks differently right? Stop that devil!

And now it's even worse in Canadian schools.

If you decide to yank your kid out of school for a couple of weeks, take them on a life-changing trip to Europe or Africa or Asia or wherever you want to go with them to discover the world, immerse them in new cultures, and what happens? The school flips its lid and dials up child services like you're some sort of fugitive on the run. WHAT THE ACTUAL FUCK, right?

Imagine this: You're trying to open your kid's eyes to the world, and the system's more concerned about them missing out on writing "c" and "e" a gazillion times until they don't look like conjoined twins. Priorities, people! I'm not shitting you, this is true stories from parents I know, all sending their kids to different Canadian schools.

And don't even get me started on the medication madness. I mean, it was already getting pretty bad in my days, but now? Might as well have a fucking pharmacy instead of a gym. Kid can't glue his butt to the chair for a mind-numbing forty-five minutes of Mrs. Dull-as-Dishwater's lecture on octagons? Bam! Slap an ADHD label on him; pump him full of pills. That'll do it! Little girl daydreaming out the window looking at the beautiful sunny day instead of drooling over grammar? Whoa there, she's got attention issues. Medicate her, stat! Or she's going nowhere in life!

It's a goddamn conveyor belt of conformity. They spot a kid who's not fitting into their tiny, rigid box of "normal," and it's like, "Alert the authorities—we've got a thinker!" Ignore the school's "friendly" suggestion to medicate your kid? Hello, child services, come check out these "unfit" parents. Again, this is no exaggeration.

Schools do call child services for this type of stuff and it's taken very seriously.

So yeah, no way in hell was I letting my kids get chewed up and spit out by that system. It's like prepping them for a life of monochrome misery, stripping away every shade of their rainbow minds, turning them into little gray-blob conformists. It's a straight-up theft of their youth, a robbery of their right to think, to question, to dream.

Every system's fucked, man, whether you're a kid or an adult. They want your kids, hook 'em young, and keep you trapped in their life-sucking cycle. It's a raw deal, and unless us dads stand up, shout "enough is enough," and take the reins, nothing's gonna change.

It's about breaking free from their chains and teaching our kids to see the world in full color, not just the grays and beiges they're being force-fed. We need to wake up, shake off the shackles, and fight for a world where living isn't just a loop of work, sleep, repeat.

I'll say it again for the record: Fuck the system.

All right, before we keep rolling with the rest of this book, let's get one thing straight: This chapter's been my personal punching bag, a spot in these pages where I've unloaded a fuckload of TMI stories and let the swear words fly like pigeons in a city square. Yeah, it might not have been a barrel of laughs like the others, or some deep, spiritual journey, or even a beacon of inspiration. That wasn't the point at all to be fair.

I'm not here trying to sell you on the "Sell Everything and Move to Mexico" dream. Even though I do believe Mexico is the new American Dream. Hell, most of you reading this, I probably wouldn't want as my neighbors anyway—no offense. And I'm definitely not suggesting you yank your kids out of school tomorrow, turn your house into Fort Knox, and drop off the grid like you're prepping for the apocalypse with thousands of cans of pickle veggies in the basement.

Nor am I saying you should ring up your doc and give him a piece of your mind about all the pills he's been pushing on your kids for a quick buck—

though, let's be real, that'd be a hell of a show, and if you do it, for the love of God, record it and send me the video so I can get a good laugh.

The point of this chapter isn't about making you do a 180 on your life choices. It's not about pushing you to some extreme. It's about cracking open a window in the echo chamber of "normal" parenting and education, letting in some fresh air. New ideas, new concepts you might not have thought about.

It's about getting you to think, to question, to maybe look at things from a different angle. It's about planting a seed, sparking a little fire in your brain that maybe, just maybe, there's another way to do this whole parenting and education gig.

Don't let the system convince you they are doing a better job at raising your kids than you would if you'd do it all without their help. You're a dadass. You can do this shit.

CHAPTER 8:

THE NANNY GIG

Emerging from the poop throne on a basic Wednesday, reeling from what I swear was the Mount Vesuvius of spicy dumps. My insides are still doing the tango, and I'm half expecting the shitter to file a fucking restraining order against me after this disaster. Staggering into the kitchen like a zombie in search of human brains, I go for a glass of cold water—my only hope to douse the internal inferno that was clearly expected after eating the spiciest Indian takeout known to men the night before. I should've known that five peppers on the menu beside the meal was only made to be eaten by true and tested, Bollywood-type Indian warriors.

As I'm fumbling with the fridge, something hits me in the corner of my eye. It's so bizarre, so utterly out of this world, that I'm spellbound, mouth agape, and the glass under the tap starts to overflow. And voila, my kitchen floor is now an impromptu stupid kiddie pool. Baby ants that had made their way inside are now enjoying a brand new water park with a free entrance. I'm cursing under my breath having to mop up this mini flood before my three-year-old, Landon, doesn't decide to reenact the slip-and-slide's banana peel wipeouts from *MarioKart N64*. It's only funny on videos when it happens to other people's kids.

What caught my eye you might ask? Jo did. Her name was Jo, but "Jo" was just the shorthand for "Jocelyne" as per her Canadian ID. Let's cut the crap, though. There's about as much chance of her being named "Jocelyne" in the heart of China, where she popped into the world in a delivery room tinier than my broom closet, sandwiched between a fish market reeking of last week's catch and a Hello Kitty backpack emporium, as there is of me winning a Nobel Prize in manners. I mean, come on, there's no way "Jocelyne" rolled off the tongue in a Mandarin conversation between mommy and daddy. It's like finding a vegan at a barbecue competition where they roast entire pigs for everyone to feast on and actually enjoy the show—possible, but you'd bet your last dollar against it.

Now, let's get one thing straight before rumors start—Jo didn't catch my eye because she was some misplaced figure in my kitchen, or some mistress I was trying to hide from my wife. Nah, she was our newly hired part-time nanny, a lifesaver thrown to two drowning parents trying to juggle crazy-busy businesses and a sequel to our baby-making adventures: another lovely boy named Skyler. After all, I fully expected her to be there, doing her thing, not cooped up in her room crafting the next great American novel via text messages to her billion cousins back in China. The lady's on the clock, for fuck sakes!

And let's not fucking mince words—Jo's looks weren't exactly causing any double-takes or sudden cardiac arrests. She wasn't the sort to strut down a runway unless it was at a "Who Ate All The

Mayonnaise Pies?" convention. Jo was this old-ish, round-ish, no-nonsense Chinese lady, barely scraping the height requirement to get on the teacup ride at Six Flags, let alone the big coasters. Anyways, if she'd get on any of these I'm sure she'd keep her resting bitch face the whole way through.

Back to the story. The earth screeches to a goddamn halt, right? I'm there, just minding my own thirsty-ass business, snatching a frosty glass of H2O, when BAM! The scene I catch in the corner of my eye hits me like a right hook from Jake Paul. Let's talk about our dear Jo, the house-help extraordinaire. Now, in the few weeks she's been bumbling around here, I swear I've only seen her munch on food like, what, once? Twice? Always the same depressing, soggy ham and cheese tragedy like she is some kind of poor high school student with the most boring parents making her lunch. But hold the phone, dude! This time, she's knee-deep in the culinary equivalent of a dumpster dive. There she is, gnawing on the skeletal remains of a rotisserie chicken that I, in my infinite laziness, left moldering in the fridge. It's fucking gross.

Jo isn't some mangy stray dog I felt sorry for and tossed a bone to. No, sir. She's supposed to be the beacon of cleanliness, the savior of our domestic chaos, not some bone-crunching goblin lurking in our kitchen for old molded shit to feast on. Yet, there she goes, chomping on those bones with the ferocity of a starved hyena, drool dripping out of her mouth and into her plate, the sound echoing in my head like a nightmarish lullaby.

But wait, it gets weirder. She's not just going to town on those bones; she's dunking them in blueberry baby puree. Yeah, you heard me. The stuff we got for little Skyler. It's like watching a car crash in slow motion—horrifying, yet you can't look away. Every crunch, every slurp, is a symphony of the grotesque. It's the kind of thing you can't unsee, no matter how hard you scrub your brain. So yeah, it was hella distracting.

The day Jo went full-on bone-gnawing savage in my kitchen was the day her nanny career at Casa de Chaos officially went down the drain. This lady's off-the-charts nutty behavior was like a big, flashing neon sign screaming, "I'm a fucking aggressive weirdo!" And after the bone-crunching horror show and traumatic memories for Landon, forcing him to wash his hair with cold water, her days were numbered.

She wasn't booted for dumpster diving in my trash—hell, I'd give her points for gross resourcefulness—but because her attitude stank worse than that old carcass she devoured. We had this picture-perfect fantasy, you know? An old Chinese lady moving in, bunch of experience with kids in her country, sprinkling her cultural fairy dust around, keeping the palace tidy, doing puzzles and origami with the ninos, teaching us to whip up rice like we own a Benihana, and turning us into chopstick-wielding ninjas. But nope, what we got was a stress bomb wrapped in disappointment. Our cultural exchange program turned into a freakin' horror show, leaving us with nothing but a bitter taste of regret and a newfound fear of chicken bones.

The thing is, hiring nannies wasn't new to us. We've had our fair share of Mary Poppins wannabes since Landon was born. But Jo? She was our first live-in experiment—and let me tell you, it was more Frankenstein than Cinderella. More Beast than Beauty. Victoria and I, being the ambitious but clueless parents we were, thought getting back to work was the move after our first kid was "old enough"—which in hindsight, was a decision loaded with more regret than a drunk texting their ex at 2 a.m. Earlier in this book, I shared with you how I feel about this issue.

We'd been through a LINEUP of nannies, each one a unique brand of terrible. But we kept searching. Why? Because I truly believe help inside your house is key if you want to be the true Dadass you are meant to be.

New parents, bless their clueless hearts, often dial up the old folks for backup with their little monsters. Why? Because granny and pappy, with their ancient wisdom and patience worn down by years of dealing with your own stupid-ass childhood shenanigans, are what most new parents consider the Navy SEALs of childcare. Plus, you turned out semi-decent, so they must've done something right. But I mentioned this earlier in the book: When my first mini-me burst onto the scene, I was a mere twenty-three-year-old immature fuck. My dick was still not full size yet, my nose was a no-mans-land for hair (ahhh the good ol' days), and my parents? They were as far from retirement as I was from getting a "World's Best Tax Filer" mug.

Now, let's drop a truth bomb with some real-deal statistics: In America, only about 60 parents of grandparents are retired by the time their grandkids are born. That's right, 40 percent of these would-be saviors are still grinding the 9-to-5, not sitting around waiting for diaper duty. So, for me, the cavalry of grandparental support? Nonexistent during weekdays and Sunday nights. My parents were both still in the thick of their boring careers, not exactly poised to jump on the babysitting bandwagon full-time.

That meant the gramps brigade was a no-show for us most of the time.

Not everyone gets a fucking battalion of nannies and grandparents to tackle the Herculean task of dealing with their poop-machine of a newborn.

Believe it or not, some warrior parents are ready to dive into the diaper-filled trenches on day fucking uno, armed only with baby wipes, a pair of fully milk-loaded boobs, and an unbreakable spirit. I'll be honest with you dude: Back when I was a spry twenty-three-year-old, I used to gaze at these parental gladiators with a mix of awe and envy. *Wow, look at them*, I'd think, *juggling a baby with the finesse of a circus performer, all without breaking a sweat or needing a single break. I wish I was that good.* I used to fantasize about having that kind of mental fortitude, ready to leap into the full-time parent role without ever whimpering for help. Because in every other situation in my life, I've never really asked for any help. Big boys don't cry, right?

But then, I got a little worldly, trotted around the globe, gained more wisdom, and had my eyes pried open. Here's the thing: Parents who end up going solo in the baby-raising Olympics—no nannies, no grandparents on speed dial, no family member lurking in the background ready to swoop in—it does not make them superhuman or even super parents for that matter. It's actually a neon-flashing sign that society's GPS is busted and we're driving down the wrong road. One too many left turns, if you catch my drift.

You see, when you take a second to look at how babies get the VIP treatment worldwide, it's a whole different ballgame. Parents are surrounded by a dream team of helpers, ensuring the little one gets the cream of the crop—the best version of their mom and dad, and it pays off.

Ever had a chick riding you, cowgirl style, and the girl's got about as much padding on her ass as a bicycle seat? I'm talking about the kind of gal whose butt is as lean as Kate Moss's midriff back in the day. Let me tell you, it's not a walk in the park. It's like signing up for a pleasure cruise and ending up on a damn horse rodeo.

And before you start picturing me as some sort of cushioned Buddha, let me set the record straight— I'm no chubby penguin waddling around with layers of blubber for protection. My hips don't have that natural cushioning, all right? So when you've got Miss Skinny-Butt going to town, it's like being on the receiving end of a jackhammer session. Each bounce feels like a direct hit to the bone with full intent of breaking them.

You might think, "Hey, any action is good action, right?" But there's a line, bro, and this is crossing it.

Well, it was my life for a few months, when I dated this chick—a tall blonde with Italian blood running hot through her veins. Our thing lasted like two or three months before she cheated on me with some French tattoo artist with an ego the size of the Empire State Building. Dodged a bullet there, if you ask me. Good riddance, right?

But during my brief stint in her world of pizzas and pasta, I got a front-row seat to the Italian family circus, especially when it comes to new babies. Her cousin popped out this little bundle of joy, a baby boy who was rocking rolls for days, looking like the Michelin Man's long-lost wine-drinking cousin.

Italians, dude, they get it. Same with Indians, Mexicans, Dominicans—a bunch of other cultures around the globe. They understand family isn't just a bunch of people who share your last name. It's this all-hands-on-deck, full-contact sport when a new baby hits the scene. New parents get swarmed with help—it's like a tactical support unit for diaper duty, meal prep, and every little thing in between. That's the fucking spirit.

Meanwhile, over here in North America, it's like we took a wrong turn at Albuquerque when it comes to family values. We're more about celebrating individual achievements than banding together for the new kid on the block. We act as if showing up to the baby shower and gifting a bottle warmer is all that's needed. It's like we've forgotten the art of rallying around the newbies, showing up, sleeves rolled up, ready to get down and dirty with baby care to ensure a positive upbringing. It's a beautiful thing, really—this communal embrace of a new life. Fucking poetic, even.

But who do we point fingers at? My favorite scapegoat—the goddamn system. It's got us so wrapped up in the rat race, we barely have time to breathe, let alone help out with a relative's newborn. It's a damn shame.

As for me? Born into a family where we're more likely to get birthday reminders from Zuckerberg's empire than from each other. The chances of my kids picking my cousins out of a lineup? Slimmer than a supermodel on, yet, another juice cleanse.

So, faced with that sad truth and recognizing the massive benefit of having extra hands on deck, we went for the rich LA parent playbook—hired a nanny. Let me tell you why I think it's the right thing to do.

All right, let's say you crunch the numbers, do a little financial jiu-jitsu, and booyah—you can afford a nanny. Now, we're not talking some Yale-educated, child psychology wizard, the kind of Mary Poppins 2.0 that'd cost you an organ or two. No, we're eyeing an experienced, down-to-earth nanny, someone who won't bleed your wallet dry. Just someone you can trust who knows how to make sure a newborn doesn't die and who doesn't eat molded chicken remains. I'm talking about a few hundred bucks a week—a deal, right?

Why so reasonable? Because you're not hiring this nanny to reinvent the wheel or to educate your kid for you. You're bringing them on board to handle the grunt work, the stuff you'd gladly trade for a root canal. The idea is to make sure that your time, limited as it sometimes painfully is, with your kiddo is all about quality, not quantity. It sucks but we're more often than not stuck in that shitty "time situation."

I handed over to my nannies the tasks I'd rather eat glass than do myself. I'm talking about the nitty-gritty, the gross work. Like dealing with poop-stained onesies—I'd sooner sign up to be a garbageman in the middle of a heatwave than tackle that nightmare. Last time I had diarrhea in my own boxers, I just threw away the fucking pair. If I would've started doing that with the onesies, I'd be broke, sucking dick for change on a busy corner. But these nannies, they're cut from a different cloth. They actually dig this lifestyle. It's like they're immune to smells and stuff.

It's like they're born to do this shit, the dirty work that makes most of us gag just thinking about it. They swoop in, all calm and collected, and tackle these horrifying tasks like they're organizing a bookshelf. It's their bread and butter.

She was not just tackling the mountain of dirty laundry—yeah, that included my sweaty gym socks, my wife's yoga pants, and the baby's latest puke-covered shirt. She was also the master chef of the household for meal prepping.

But wait, there's more. She was on bottle duty, too. Prepping those milk bottles for the graveyard shift was her specialty. It's easy stuff, but it's the tiny details like that that accumulate and help a whole lot. So when you're yanked out of a perfectly good wet dream by the ear-piercing wails of your mini-you, you're not fumbling around like a zombie trying to figure out the milk-to-water ratio. It's grab, warm, and serve—a streamlined process that allows you to handle the whole situation more calmly, and that's good for you and for baby.

These might sound like small victories, but man, they're game-changers. It's about shaving off those extra layers of stress, those little annoyances that pile up and turn your days and nights into dumpster fires.

And let's not forget about the other godsend tasks nannies handle. We're talking about turning the chaos of toy landmines in the living room into a place where you can actually see the fucking floor. They're like magical fairies, whisking away the clutter, leaving behind a space that doesn't look like a category 5 hurricane just ripped through it.

For me, having a nanny was all about sanity-saving.

In short, the nanny isn't just helping—she's practically co-piloting this crazy ride of parenting. You still have all control, you still make all major decisions, but if you need to take a nap, the plane won't crash.

All right, let's cut the crap and stop tossing bouquets at nannies for a sec. Yeah, they're great, they're lifesavers, yada yada, but deep down, I wish I didn't have to shell out cash for this kind of help. It was either a trip to Cuba in an all-inclusive or the nanny for a year so the choice was easy, but still, it's money leaving the pockets. I mean, wouldn't it be sweet if my mom was one of those badass Mexican abuelas, dedicating her golden years to spoiling my kids rotten? But that's not my deck of cards, and it's probably not yours either.

So, if you're about to dive into the nanny hiring pool, aiming to ease your life and step up your dadass game, there are a few things you gotta watch out for. It's not all sunshine and rainbows; there are some rotten apples in this field.

Number 1) Make sure she doesn't have young kids of her own. Why? Two fucking good reasons.

First up, it's about damn priorities. Your kid needs to be top of the list when she's on the clock. It's harsh but true. You can't—and shouldn't—expect any mom to put your kid before her own flesh and blood. That's just twisted. Like a weird mental game from *Saw*. And think about it: She spends all day pouring her energy into your little one, then goes home and snaps at her own kid because she's running on empty? Hell no. That's the kind of shit that hits you right back with karma. I've got a selfish streak, sure, but that's crossing a line I'm not willing to toe.

Also, kids are like walking petri dishes, man. They're always catching something, especially in those early years. A cold, gastro, whatever you name it. If she's got young ones, you can bet all your bitcoins she'll be calling in sick more often than a high schooler with senioritis. Every sniffle, every cough her kid gets, it's a ticking time bomb for your schedule and for your kid to get it was well.

You need reliability, consistency. You can't be playing roulette with your nanny's availability.

Number 2) Check her social media use. The less, the merrier. You can't physically grab her phone and check all the apps she's on, but you can and should ask during the interview. Yeah, I might sound like some crusty old dude yelling at clouds and calling all birds government drones, but hear me out. The last thing—and I mean the very last thing—you want is to leave your kid with her, dash out for like ten minutes for some dish soap, and come back to find her TikToking away, doing some retarded dance challenge with your baby as a prop.

Let's get real—there's something about these TikTok-addicted kids that just scrambles their brains like eggs at a Sunday brunch. It's like they lose the part that's responsible for sound judgment. One minute they're supposed to be babysitting, the next, they're auditioning for internet fame with your kid as an unwilling co-star. Fuck that.

Number 3) Does she have some muscle on her, or is she about as sturdy as a wet noodle? I'm not saying she needs to be bench-pressing cars like Wonder Woman or looking like she'd stand a chance in a cage fight against Conor McGregor. But let's be real: Nanny work is no walk in the park. It can and will get her sweaty.

You've got to consider the physical aspect of the job. Can she handle a flight of stairs without huffing and puffing like she's smoking during a marathon? When she's cradling your little bundle of joy, is she gonna tap out after five minutes because her arms are shaking like a leaf in a tornado?

And think about the housework, man. Sweeping, mopping—that's not for the faint of heart. You need someone who can handle a mop like a pro, not someone who's gonna throw out their back at the sight of a dirty floor.

So how do you figure out if she's up for the physical challenge of being your nanny? Simple:

Put her to the test. Hand her a pair of fifteen-pound dumbbells and fire up a fifteen-minute HIIT workout on YouTube. Watch her go at it. If she can keep up without looking like she's about to pass out, you might just have a winner.

Number 4) Last but not least, let's talk about one more crucial piece of the ideal perfect nanny puzzle: her lifestyle habits. Because, let's face it, experience and a positive attitude are extremely important—that just goes without saying. But if she's living like a sixth member of the Rolling Stones off-duty, you're in for a world of pain.

Imagine this: You've got a nanny who's more familiar with the bottom of a liquor bottle than the children's section at the library. She stumbles in, reeking of last night's mistakes at the local tavern, trying to hold down her breakfast at the mere whiff of a dirty diaper. And we all know there's a lot of those in a day.

And then there's also the Marlboro woman, puffing away like she's got a personal vendetta against her lungs. Competition between both lungs to see which one will turn black first. You don't want to turn your home into a makeshift ashtray, constantly lighting incense like you're running a hippie commune, just to mask the stench of her chain-smoking habit.

You've got to safeguard not just your kid, but the whole vibe of your home. It's your sanctuary, dude. You can't let someone waltz in with their self-destructive habits, polluting the air—both literally and figuratively. This isn't just about protecting your kid's physical health; it's about maintaining the energy of your space.

Basically, you need someone who's not just there to watch your kid but also to contribute to a healthy, positive environment.

So, you get this nanny on board, right? And suddenly, your time with your kid isn't about scrubbing stains or battling the laundry monster. It's about the good stuff—playing, laughing, teaching, being present. It's like outsourcing the chaos so you can zero in on the magic of being a dad. A pure fucking dadass.

That's the beauty of having a nanny. It's not just about getting help; it's about reshaping your role as a parent.

It allows you to also take more time for yourself to become a better human overall.

I did just that recently. I got out of my comfort zone to figure out some shit about me, face my demons to come back as a better dad.

The first help I needed was a nanny, to give me the time and space to leave.

The second help I needed was from this tiny thing we call...mushrooms.

CHAPTER 9:

HIPPIE DADDY

Man, for a second I swear the man looked like this beast that seemed to have leaped straight off a heavy metal album cover. The kind of shit only creepy artists with very dark thoughts can come up with. I mean, picture this: a creature with a fucking huge deer's head, like it had raided Santa's stash of steroids, equipped with a sharp stack on blood-covered shark's teeth, slapped onto the body of a ghostly tall white horse straight out of a gothic horror flick. And those pointy wings—man, they weren't just regular wings; they were like dragon wings, the kind that would make Daenerys Targaryen green with envy.

Our hearts were pounding like we'd just downed ten espressos and a king-size Red Bull. Anxiety was creeping up on us faster than a taxman on payday, even though this mythical Harry Potter-type monster didn't seem keen on turning us into its next meal. But, come on, you don't just casually bump into a creature like that and expect to walk away like it's a Sunday stroll in the park. It was obviously looking for some fresh teenage blood.

What if this thing tried to communicate? What if it started spouting some intergalactic gibberish because it comes straight from a hellish planet in another fucked up galaxy, and we accidentally ticked it off by just standing there, dumbfounded? I had this insane image of it rearing up like a circus horse gone rogue, flapping those gargantuan wings and whipping up a record-breaking tornado right there. Imagine being sucked up into a whirlwind, spun around like laundry in an evil dryer, and then flung thousands of kilometers away. Our poor families would be left to piece together what happened from the jigsaw puzzle of our remains, scattered across some godforsaken forest in the middle of buttfuck nowhere.

So here's the kicker: This mind-bending, nightmare-fueling mystical monstrosity that made us all almost shit our pants? Turns out it was just some regular forties-ish Joe, probably named Bob or something equally basic, who was out for a peaceful midnight jaunt in the national park like a good healthy citizen. Yeah, just a random fucking guy probably wondering if he had left his stove on, accidentally stumbling upon a ragtag bunch of six dudes tripping so hard they were practically in another galaxy in the middle of the woods.

Imagine this guy's surprise. One minute he's enjoying the crickets and night breeze, asking himself how he's going to admit to his wife that he didn't get the promotion he'd promised her he'd get so they could buy that cute little cottage they'd visited four times last spring, and the next, he's the unwitting star of a hallucinogenic horror show. We probably freaked him out more than he did us. I wouldn't be surprised if he sprinted home to write his own survival horror story, or just fucking called the cops at that point. I wouldn't blame him.

Let's talk about why our brains decided to turn this innocent hiker into a creature that looked like it had escaped from a Guillermo del Toro film during what was my first magic mushroom experience. It's all about the headspace, man. We were already slowly entering the psychedelic soup, when our minds started doing the salsa with darkness and paranoia. All because of one female cop who was, in our view, at the wrong place, wrong time.

I was probably seventeen years young. I can guess the age based on what I remember being my experience in the vagina action department. At that time, it was so scarce I could've listed it on a Post-it note. I was living under my parents' roof, where my most risqué adventure was sneaking an extra cookie from the jar after dinner and smoking weed through a toilet paper roll with a Bounce sheet at the end to cover the smell near the bathroom window. But hey, I was already a stoner of such caliber that I found "Austin Powers" to be the peak of cinematic excellence—and let me tell you, that's a whole different level of baked. If you don't agree that's fine, I'm not here to judge your taste in movies. But Austin Powers movies are a 6/10, at best—fight me.

It was just another sleepy Wednesday in Saint-Hyacinthe, where the most exciting event was probably Mrs. Tremblay's fat orange cat getting stuck in a tree again. But for me and my band of misfit nerds, it was gearing up to be a trippy odyssey for the ages. We started by all meeting up at the oldest dude's apartment. The plan? A Super Smash Bros. tournament on N64.

Here's the scene that probably most dudes my age experienced: Six dudes, five of whom still had their bedrooms decked out in teenage angst and band posters in their parents' basement, huddled around a TV. Peak male activity, right? The tournament was going about as well as you'd expect for me—a guy whose gaming prowess was usually limited to beating my big sister and occasionally my younger brother if he got the malfunctioning controller. My parents were not allowing me to play video games enough for me to become an unbeatable machine compared to all my nerdy-ass friends. On top of that, my go-to character, Fox, was snagged by my buddy Hamza, leaving me with Link. No disrespect to Link, but let's be real: He wasn't my first, second, or even third choice. The sword is cool and all, but I didn't vibe the character.

After guzzling enough sugary juices and energy drinks and a couple beers, we decided it was time to up the ante: magic mushrooms. The plan was to sneak into the national park under the cover of darkness, because apparently, we thought there would be fewer people, if any, to witness our ascension to the other dimension.

Now, the method of shroom consumption that night? Yogurt. Why yogurt, you ask? Beats me. It wasn't my brainwave. But the guys seemed convinced this was the gourmet way to trip balls. The guys seemed pretty confident they knew what they were doing, so I followed along thinking to myself that they probably had done their research on the subject prior to that night. So I just went with it and swallowed mine whole in two spoonfuls.

How much did we take? If my now-seasoned shroom expertise is worth anything, I'd wager it was somewhere between 1.5 to 2.0 grams each, ballpark. That's the sweet spot—enough to send you on a visual roller coaster, with the world morphing around you like some psychedelic kaleidoscope. You know, have a good time, but not so much that you're diving headfirst into a soul-searching, trauma-healing, alien-handshaking odyssey that changes the way you perceive life on this planet.

The game plan was all laid out and fairly simple: wolf down those mushroom-infused yogurt cups in under five minutes, put on shoes and jackets, and make a beeline for the park. It was only a ten-minute drive, a perfect buffer before the shrooms started their magic. We figured we'd get there with plenty of time to stake out a cozy spot under the stars, lay back, and let the trip gently roll in like a fog.

Unfortunately for us, as we got out of the apartment and found ourselves crammed like sardines into a '99 Toyota Corolla, six dudes on a mission for a cosmic trip, ready to embrace the night's epic adventures, bam! Just as we were rolling out, police lights started flashing in front of us, slicing through the darkness like a bad omen. And wouldn't you know it, the cop car pulled up right in front of us. Talk about a buzzkill.

Now, let me make one thing fucking clear, I've got no beef with female cops. There, I said it. In fact, I'm all for gender diversity in the police force. Men and women bring different perspectives to the table, and that balance is crucial for a police force that's truly for the people. But that night, having a woman officer pull us over right as we were about to embark on our shroom journey? It was like being a kid again, trying to sneak past mom after smoking a joint, the smell of guilt practically wafting off you.

You know that feeling, right? You don't want to let mom down, but you also want to enjoy your high. There's this awkward dance of trying to act normal, but inside, you're a mess of paranoia and dread. That's exactly how it felt facing that officer.

At that moment, the boys and I all felt like Eminem in *8 Mile* before the rap battle. Palms were sweaty, knees weak, arms heavy—nervous. On the surface we looked calm and ready to drop bombs, but we kept forgetting what we had written down. We opened our mouths but the words wouldn't come out. Okay, enough. Mom's spaghetti.

That's it, I'm done. Back to the story.

Two things to remember in this scene: It was as dark as the depths of space outside (okay, maybe not, but dark as shit), which was part of our master plan. The cover of night was supposed to be our ally on this shroom escapade. But now, it was working against us, with this cop shining her flashlight into our car like she was on some kind of treasure hunt. Every beam of light felt like it was searing right through me, cranking my anxiety up to eleven. Sure, I had nothing to hide, but there was something about being under the cop microscope that made my skin crawl. You know, me and authority...it's not a love story.

Then, second thing, there was the ticking time bomb of the shrooms. Every second this cop spent grilling us was a second closer to the whole carful of us blasting off into the stratosphere. The last thing any of us needed was to start tripping balls with a cop right outside the window. Especially in a car driven by a nineteen-year-old school dropout tripping.

So, the pressure was on. The idea of him navigating the streets while the shrooms were doing their magic? That was a recipe for disaster. I had no intention of dying this young. There was so much more I wanted to do in life before calling it a day.

We needed to get out of this situation, pronto, before the psychedelic storm hit full force.

Quick thinking, a solid story—that's what we needed. Something believable, something to get this cop off our backs so we could hightail it to the park and ride out the trip in peace.

Diving into the past for this book—for you, bro—has been like navigating a jungle of memories. I'm all about keeping it real, no sugarcoating, no bullshitting. The stories, the lessons, the raw truths of this book—they're all tied up in my personal experiences, so accuracy is key. I'm not a fucking liar so my stories have to be true, no modifications. But here's the thing: When it comes to that night with the cops and the shrooms, I can recall almost everything, but unfortunately my memory's as clear as mud for that exact part.

What was our get-out-of-jail-free card? Did we play the "sick friend" angle, cutting our wild night short to play the good Samaritans who had to bring our homie back to his house for some soup? Or did we spin some yarn about needing to move the car for apartment renovations announced late night by the property owner? It's a haze, a swirling fog of "What the hell did we say?" The details are lost in the psychedelic ether.

That's why it's all a blur: I was the first one to wolf down that shroom-infused yogurt by the spoonfuls. And let me tell you, they kicked in like a mule in my frail, little 125-pound teenager body. So, as that cop was making her way back to her cruiser, something wild started happening. The car seat beneath me began to shift and sway, and suddenly, it felt like we were not just driving—we were flying.

Let me lay it down easy for you: That night, with the shrooms taking hold in the midst of our cop-induced anxiety, everything took a dark turn from that point until the very end of the experience. Our heightened nerves set the stage for the trip, and boy, did it follow the script. Every shadow seemed sinister, every noise had an eerie edge, and every moment was tinged with a surreal, stressful vibe that we couldn't fucking shake off. It was a psychedelic horror show, and we were the unwitting stars.

There's a reason why I'm spilling this tale at the start of this chapter. Psychedelics, man, they're not just some recreational joyride. They can be, but that's not why we're here in the first place. You picked up this book because you care about becoming a badass dad. So mushrooms, in this case, have a different intention. They're a tool, a key to unlocking parts of your mind you never knew existed. They can open doors to new perspectives, new ways of thinking, new patterns of behavior. But here's the catch—they're like a genie in a bottle, and you better be damn sure about your wish before you let it out.

The golden rule of any psychedelic journey, and it's especially true when taking them in a ceremonial practice, is setting an intention. It's like programming your GPS before you hit the road. That intention is your guide, your north star, through the twists and turns of your mind. Without it, you're just a leaf in the wind, tossed around by the whims of your subconscious. And unfortunately, that might lead you nowhere good…or nowhere at all.

Let's fast forward and dive into my re-entry into the world of magic mushrooms, eleven years later, through the use of microdosing—something that's become as trendy as having a string of pronouns in sunny California. Me? I'm just a guy who's always on the hunt for self-improvement, constantly looking for that next level-up in personal development. That's when I stumbled upon the whole microdosing scene. That first terrifying experience at seventeen was my last time touching them, but there was something extremely appealing, interesting, and science based about microdosing that put me at ease.

We're talking about studies, loads of them, singing praises about the benefits of microdosing shrooms for your brain. It's like finding a cheat code for mental wellness. No joke. At this point, I'm on a mission to amp up my patience. Let's be real, I'm sometimes about as patient as a kid on Christmas Eve. I mean, there are these moments, I'm not fucking proud of them, but like waiting for that gas station guy to set the pump to 800 pesos, where I'm seconds away from turning the pump hose into a makeshift lasso and strangle the damn shit out of him. How the hell can it take ten minutes from the moment I tell you how much gas I need and you putting the freaking thing in my car?

I did microdosing for a solid three months. It was a regimen of one day on, one day off—the classic recommended approach for most. Now, let's get one thing straight: I'm about as far from a naturopath as you can get. Everything I know, I know from my wife. Because my wife, well, she's got the creds. So, with her guidance, I had a pretty good handle on the dosages and the whole "brain reprogramming" gig I was looking for. But hey, everyone's wired differently, so if you're thinking about giving microdosing a chance, do yourself a favor and chat with a professional. Not a fucking generic doctor who knows sweet fuck all about this stuff. I'm talking a naturopath ideally so she can craft a plan that fits your unique wiring and help you obtain the best results possible.

Consider this my disclaimer, my "don't try this at home without expert advice" warning label. I gotta keep it vague on the specifics of quantities, partly because I don't want any of you chasing me down with lawsuits, claiming I messed up your wiring and now because of microdosing you're suddenly into midget porn. I'm not calling anyone a dummy, but let's not forget the Tide Pod fiasco—a stark reminder that common sense isn't always as common as you'd expect. So, yeah, covering my bases here because, as it turns out, the world's got its fair share of knuckleheads who can't think for themselves one second.

Now that my ass is legally covered, I hope, let's talk about how microdosing nudged me way closer to dadass territory. It wasn't some overnight transformation, no "Eureka!" moment. It was more like fine-tuning an old radio, getting rid of the static bit by bit until it sounds better than ever.

Okay, so here's the way this microdosing thing actually works. When you're microdosing mushrooms, you're playing the long game with your brain. You're tapping into the benefits of psilocybin without signing up for a full-blown psychedelic adventure. So, don't be a little crybaby, and get scared about popping your microdose with your morning brew and then finding yourself in some trippy, Technicolor dreamland, grooving with the trees while John Lennon serenades you from the clouds with "imagine all the people." That's not the microdosing script. That's macrodosing.

When you get microdosing right, it's subtle. You're not going to feel some earth-shattering shift each time you take your dose. It's not a "whoa, dude, I'm fucking flying" moment; it's more of a "huh, neat" kind of deal. For the first couple of months, it was like that for me—no fireworks, just a gentle nudge here and there in my brain. The best way I could describe the immediate effects was "clarity."

But then, month three rolls around, and I decide to crank it up a notch, double the dosage but still remaining under the umbrella of microdosing. Suddenly, I'm noticing this new sensation I hadn't felt before. It's like my internal thermostat gets a bit wonky for about half an hour after dosing. I'm feeling a bit warmer, a little flushed, but nothing to write home about. It's not like I'm sweating bullets or anything.

This is the thing about microdosing—it's not about the immediate buzz because that's not what we're after. It's a slow burn, a gradual rewiring and fine-tuning of the gray matter upstairs. You're not going to see the effects in vibrant colors or wild hallucinations. It's happening under the hood, in the engine room of your mind.

Think of it like planting a garden. You don't see the flowers blooming right away. You water it, give it sunlight, and over time, you start to see the growth, the changes. That's microdosing. You're planting seeds in your brain, through an intention (like mine was about becoming a more patient father) watering them with these tiny doses of psilocybin, and eventually, you start to notice the shifts—the new sprouts of creativity, patience, or whatever you're aiming to cultivate. On the microdosing days, things just seemed a bit...smoother. It was like my brain had a fresh coat of paint. Ideas came easier, patience wasn't as elusive, and my fuse...well, it got a little longer. It's not like I turned into Mr. Zen, meditating on a mountaintop, levitating like fucking monk wizard. But there was a shift, a gentle nudge toward being a more chilled-out, creative, in-the-moment kind of guy. Who wasn't worried about what would come next.

The biggest win? My quest for patience. In the throes of fatherhood, patience isn't just a virtue; it's your best freaking friend. Microdosing gave me a taste of that, a sneak peek into a calmer, more collected version of myself. I knew a patient dad was inside of me. I just needed to show it some love and let it out.

Now scientifically speaking, for all you science nerds out there, here's the geeky bit about microdosing. Recent studies—and I'm talking legit, respected-in-the-scientific-community kind of studies—have shown some pretty mind-blowing stuff that confirms exactly the results I had. When you microdose psilocybin, over time, with a plan and a clear intention, it's like giving your brain a power-up. The compounds in psilocybin boost the density of dendritic spines. These little guys are the protrusions on nerve cells that help neurons chat with each other. In layman's terms, it's like building new highways between your brain cells.

And let me tell you, you can feel this happening. It's like your brain is quietly working in the background, re-routing traffic. Especially in those moments when you usually react in ways you're not exactly proud of, you start to notice a shift. It's as if your brain's got a mind of its own, realizing there might be a better route to take, a different way to process and react to situations.

Now, why does this matter? Because chronic stress and depression, those sneaky sons of a bitch, saboteurs of your dadass status, they do a number on these neuronal connections. They're like roadblocks, clogging up the pathways in your brain. And let's face it, us guys? We're often stress magnets, walking around like we've got the weight of the world on our shoulders. It's no wonder our reactions can sometimes be shitty.

That's why I felt it was so important for me to write about my experience with microdosing. I'm not saying it's a silver bullet, a cure-all for every mental hang-up. And it's definitely not a substitute for therapy or working through your issues the old-fashioned way. But as a step, a tool in your self-improvement thing? It's worth giving it a solid try. It's also not something you get fucking addicted to. You won't become a mushroom junkie needing a fix so no worries there. And these new pathways don't stop working when you stop your microdosing plan. They instill permanent changes that make you a better human.

So, does dabbling in microdosing shrooms make me some kind of modern-day tattooed hippie? And you know what? If that's the case, I'm not even that mad about it. Few thing thought that not fit the stereotypical "hippie" mold in my life—I'm all about personal hygiene, for starters . I'm the guy who takes daily showers with organic soap (none of that chemical-laden shit), keeps the hair, beard, pubes, back, and chest trimmed. But hey, embracing a bit of that hippie mindset that so many amazing parents had in the '60s and '70s? It's not looking too shabby from where I'm standing, to be honest with you.

The more I dove into the world of psychedelics, the more I started rethinking the whole '70s hippie stereotype. I started reading more and more about the mindset and ideology of these times and I can't say I wasn't impressed. Society's got this image of them as these aimless, underachieving slackers. "Losers" would be the main terminology. But let's hit pause and give credit where it's due. Those guys were onto something with their mind-expanding trips. They were pioneers, in a way, using psychedelics to crack open the doors of perception. Break away from the box society is trying to put us all in.

It's funny how perspectives shift. Here I am, a dad trying to be the best version of himself, and I find myself walking a path that these so-called "losers" blazed decades ago. They were experimenting with psychedelics, exploring consciousness, challenging norms—all in the pursuit of enlightenment, or at least a different way of seeing the world and raising kids to be amazing open-minded people with loads of respect for the environment and each other.

So, yeah, maybe there's a bit of hippie in me after all. And I'm okay with that. If using mushrooms as a tool to level up my dadass game, to expand my mind and improve my patience, puts me in that category, then so be it. It doesn't mean I'm about to ditch showers and start listening to The Doors on loop. But it does mean I'm open to exploring unconventional paths to personal growth.

And I did just that one year after incorporating microdosing in my lifestyle, when I revisited a macrodose. And bro…it changed everything.

There's this saying back home that goes, "Quebecers are always everywhere. You could be standing on top of Mount Everest, soaking in the epic view, and in the distance, you'll hear: *"Ginette, t'a tu amenée la camera? Prend donc une photo d'moe la."* Go ahead, toss that into Google Translate if you're curious. It's spot on, and man, does it crack me up. Mostly because it's so damn true.

Now, I'm not what you'd call a serious globetrotter, mainly because traveling these days means buying four damn plane tickets instead of just one. And holy shit does it hit the wallet like a ton of bricks. But I've had my fair share of adventures around the world—Italy, France, Colombia, Mexico, the U.S., Costa Rica, Russia, Switzerland, the U.K., and a few others that slip my mind. Not too bad for a thirty-year-old dude who was once stealing sandwiches to survive.

And everywhere I've gone, not once have I managed to escape my fellow Quebecers. It's like they've got a homing beacon for me. I could be in the most random little café in Rome, a tucked-away restaurant in Medellin, or some out-of-the-way gas station in Moscow, and bam—I'll run into someone from Quebec who's complaining about either the temperature or the price of things. It's like we're a swarm of locusts, descending on every corner of the globe.

Don't get me wrong, I like some things about my Quebec roots, but come on, can a guy get a break from the mother tongue for just a bit? It's like no matter how far you go, how exotic or remote the place, you're bound to bump into someone who's probably your third cousin twice removed or knows your Aunt Diane.

It's hilarious and a bit surreal. You leave Quebec, hoping to experience a new culture, hear different languages, and there you are, ordering a cappuccino, and the guy next to you asks in thick Quebecois French if you know a good poutine spot in town. It's a small world, sure, but for us Quebecers, it seems even smaller. To top it off, here in the south of Mexico, there's a huge community of Quebecer expats. All more annoying than the other. In the midst of dodging tank top and pit viper-wearing Quebecers left and right—you know, the kind who make you cringe so hard you could pull a face muscle—I actually stumbled upon this one cool chick. She's gone full expat, married a Mexican dude, had babies, and now owns this adorable little Airbnb resort smack dab in the heart of Tulum. Talk about living the dream.

My wife on Instagram has this intense magnetism—like how a rotten banana in the sun pulls in fruit flies from miles away. She's a social media sorceress or something. Well, because of her Insta-fame, and our cool personalities, this Tulum queen offers us a private cabana for a full day and a night. And not just any night—we're talking about the perfect setting for a full-on, no-holds-barred macrodose of mushrooms. A psychedelic ceremony in paradise? With my wife? Both setting intentions to become better parents and lovers? Holy shit, sign me up!

Victoria, being the absolute white wizard that she is, transformed our little cabana into what can only be described as a cozy, inviting sanctuary. We're talking blankets spread out like a sea of comfort on the floor, surrounded by an army of pillows. There was fresh water in glasses glinting in the dim light, crystals scattered about like treasures, spreading some grounding energy, and the lights dialed down to just the right level of ambiance. Honestly, it would be the perfect set-up for a night of Kamasutra positions in which both of us cum more than once, but that's not on tonight's schedule. The stage is set for a deep dive into the psyche.

But let's not kid ourselves; I'm nervous as hell. I'm still wrestling with a couple of heavyweights in my mind. First off, there's the lingering trauma from that wild night back in 2010. What fresh evil shit could unfold this time? Will the ceiling fan morph into a demonic, blood-sucking serpent? Or maybe, just as we're about to embark on our spiritual journey, some mustachioed five-foot-one Mexican cop might crash the party, guns drawn, over a couple trying to level up in the parenting game. But I had to stop thinking about all that jazz. I was in a safe place.

Then there's the second reason, the big one that holds so many people back from even flirting with psychedelics: good old-fashioned fear. Fear of the journey, of what the mushrooms might drag out of the dark corners of your mind. When you're gearing up for a macrodose with the intention of growth, you're basically signing up for a mental boot camp. The shrooms are going to hold up a mirror to your soul, and they're not always gentle about it. Sure, it's all in the name of coming out the other side a better person, but let's be real—when you're in the thick of it, it can be a rough ride you weren't prepared for.

My nerves were buzzing like a hive of bees, knowing that I needed to simmer down to get the most out of this experience. I knew too well that going into it nervous wouldn't make this easy. Victoria, being the intuitive genius she is, sensed this. She guided me to sit down and kick off a guided breathwork session.

In through the nose, out through the mouth— it's a rhythm as old as time, but damn, does it work wonders when you actually take the time to do it properly. Fifteen minutes of this focused meditative breathwork, and I was as chill as a cucumber in a freezer. Seriously, I was so mellow at this point, I could stroll into a colonoscopy and crack jokes with the doc as he's inserting the camera right up my stinker. Breathwork, man—I already mentioned in this book how it's like this secret weapon for reining in the wild horses of my emotions. Especially in moments like this, when the nerves are trying to run the show, a good deep-breathing session is like hitting the reset button.

As we wrapped up the breathing sesh, I could feel every muscle in my body just letting go, releasing the tension that had been coiling up inside. It was the perfect prelude to what was about to come. I took my dose of mushrooms, the magic ticket for the night's enlightenment, and got myself all set up. I slipped on a thick blindfold, adding an extra layer of sensory deprivation to the mix. That way I could focus on what was going inside instead of being distracted by the outside. Then, I lay back, my head finding the sweet spot on my pillow, arms relaxed by my sides, palms facing up to the universe as if to say, "I'm ready, bring it on."

Lying there, in the heart of our makeshift ceremonial space, I felt like an astronaut about to launch into the unknown. Every sense was heightened, every nerve ending was buzzing with anticipation for what I hoped to be a life-changing ceremony. The blindfold plunged me into darkness, a blank canvas for the psychedelic symphony that was about to play out in my mind. Would I revisit and heal childhood traumas? Would I finally understand my fear of shower walls? Or would it stick to my intention and open my mind to new ways of parenting?

It was a strange mix of peace and excitement, like standing on the edge of a cliff, ready to dive into an ocean of consciousness. I was at the mercy of the mushrooms, surrendering to whatever they had in store for me. It was a leap of faith, a trust fall into the arms of the universe.

Words barely do justice to the mad cascade of experiences and revelations that unfolded during that ceremony. As a grown man, setting foot into this psychedelic realm in a safe space, with the love of my life and with clear intentions, I was primed for something profound, but what I got was beyond any expectation.

The journey kicked off with me tumbling down an actual rabbit hole, and I'm not just throwing metaphors around here. It was like I'd been plucked straight out of reality and dropped into a scene from *Alice in Wonderland*, but without the evil, creepy fat cat. Down and down I went, deeper into this endless spiral, and as I was falling, my life started flashing before my eyes. But it was not like a movie reel; it was more immersive, more intense. And to my surprise, it was all scenes that made me smile. All of it was mostly artistic shit I had done since I first realized as a kid that I saw beauty in all types of art. I know it sounds kind of sissy but it's true.

Imagine you're on one of those rides at Disneyland, where they hand you 3D glasses and plop you into a rickety car on squeaky rails. Except in my head, I was not just a spectator; I was living it, breathing it. It was a multi-sensory overload, like being in the middle of the *Ratatouille* movie ride at the Paris Disney park, surrounded by a whirlwind of culinary chaos and a corny horde of animated rats.

I was grinning like a madman, laughing till my sides hurt, and bawling like a baby who had lost his favorite pacifier. All at once sometimes. Pretty fucked up. But when the dust settled, when the last happy tear had rolled down my cheek, there it was—this massive, kick-you-in-the-balls realization that I was secretly hoping for from this whole shroom shindig.

Let's get real here: I didn't just waltz into this ceremony expecting some divine epiphany to smack me upside the head. I knew there was a fat chance my stubborn-ass ego could play gatekeeper, blocking the deep shit from really sinking in right away. Hell, I was half-expecting to need weeks, maybe months, of brain-wrangling meditation to decode whatever cryptic message the shrooms decided to toss my way.

But lo and behold, the universe must've been feeling generous, 'cause the message hit me with the subtlety of a sledgehammer the moment I propped myself up and yanked off that blindfold: "Business Dad" needs a freakin' vacation. It's high time to introduce the kiddos to a dude they've barely met— "Artist Dad."

That's right, it was like the shrooms were screaming, "Hey, numbnuts, you've been so wrapped up in starting brands, building networks, the never-ending quest for more money that you've forgotten there's more to you than just being a business-savvy, cool young dad. You've got this whole other side, this creative, artsy-fartsy part that's been gathering dust in the corner of your brain." I've been a fucking artist all my life and now I let the appeal of blazer and ties take the best of me.

And damn, did that realization feel like a breath of fresh air. It's like I'd been playing this one-note tune for so long, I forgot I had a whole damn symphony in me. The "Artist Dad"—he's the guy who's gonna show the kids that life isn't just about deadlines and dollar signs. It's about splashing paint on a canvas, strumming a guitar till your fingers ache, and dancing in the living room like nobody's watching. To just live your dreams and see where it fucking leads you.

I firmly believe every adult, especially every parent, oughta roll up their sleeves and dive headfirst into a macrodose of magic mushrooms. Not every goddamn week but at least once. And I'm talking about doing it right—in a safe, ceremonial setting where you can really let the experience wash over you . For me, it's become as routine as taking the damn family car in for an oil change and tire alignment. Since that first eye-opener in Tulum, I've been hitting the shroom ceremonies about thrice a year, and let me tell you, it's a game-changer.

Wanna hear something wild? The idea for this book, the whole shebang of pages you've been going through, hit me like a ton of bricks during a mushroom trip on the sandy shores of Puerto Escondido. Inspiration started flowing through me like a damn firehose just hours after the peak of the experience had passed. I was scribbling down ideas like a madman. Sure, not all of it was gold—some of it was pure gibberish that I would rate a solid 3/10—but bits and pieces of those trippy musings made their way into every chapter of this book. It's like the shrooms tapped into a part of my brain that's usually on snooze mode.

Each ceremony is like a personal revolution. I come out the other side with new insights, new ideas, tearing down the walls my ego's been busy building. It's a chance to try new stuff, to step out of the comfort zone. And in this case, it led to something pretty damn cool—writing a book. And not just any book, but one I'm fucking proud of.

We always say life's short, right? It zips by in the blink of an eye, especially when you're a parent. Your brain's like a 24/7 kid-focused machine, constantly worrying about their needs, their future. You want to be a cool dad, a pure dadass, but it's easy to get lost in the sauce, drowning in stress and anxiety, busting your ass just to keep the lights on and the kids in new sneakers. But here's the million-dollar question: Does that mean you gotta kiss your dreams goodbye?

Hell no.

That's the beauty of these mushroom trips. They're like a slap behind the head, a wake-up call reminding you that there's more to life than just being "Dad." It's about rediscovering yourself, reigniting those dreams and passions that got buried under a mountain of diapers and PTA meetings.

The most badass thing you can do as a father, the ultimate power move, is staying true to yourself. It's about not letting the grind of life squash your mojo, not letting the daily hustle snuff out your spark. Show your kids what it means to chase happiness, to try new stuff, to hustle for your dreams, live your passions. That's the kind of legacy that'll light a fire under their butts, the kind of inspiration that turns your mini-mes into mini-mavericks.

Now, I wouldn't be surprised if, right at this moment, you're furiously texting your contacts for a shroom hookup in your town or deep-diving into Google in search of some magic mushroom emporium that delivers in the next 24h. If you've stuck with me this far, hats off to you. I'm stoked. Why? Because even if it's just a flicker, a tiny spark in the back of your mind, this chapter might've just kicked open the door to a whole new world for you.

Think about it. Maybe, just maybe, you're on the brink of trying something wild, something that shakes up the status quo. You could be one step away from rewiring your brain, from ditching those crusty old habits that your ego's been hoarding like a packrat. Those habits, man, they're like ankle weights, dragging you down, holding you back from reaching peak dadass status.

Or maybe you think I'm just a hippie who's losing it. In that case, well, go to hell (just kidding).

CHAPTER 10:

GO FOR ONE MORE ROUND?

All right, let's set the record straight once and for all. The number of dudes who've had the, let's say, "honor" of eyeballing my manhood up close and personal? Pretty damn low. Sure, there might've been a few accidental glimpses from creeps at the urinal, or maybe some fortunate driving souls caught a peek when I had to pull over for an emergency roadside leak (which to be honest happens fairly often). But a full-on, in-your-face viewing of my dick? Nah, that's a club with exclusive women-only membership.

Now, when it comes to actual hands-on experience, the list is even shorter and almost single gender except these very few exceptions. Childhood memories aside, with my old man and grandpa dealing with the typical baby mess, there's really just one guy who didn't earn a swift uppercut or kidney kick for copping a feel of the family jewels. And this dude, he's not just some random guy. This legend, believe it or not, follows me on Instagram, and I even follow him back. Yeah, we're that close now. That shit's special.

Thing is, he didn't even get what all women who touched it called "the pleasure of handling the full monty, the blood-engorged rock-hard beast" itself. That would've been way beyond awkward, considering his job was just to nudge it out of the way. Just a quick flip up against my belly to get clear access to the star of the show, my nutsack, all prepped and freshly shaved with a dash of mint aftershave for the big event. You've probably put the pieces together by now—this man, this brave soul, was the doc who sealed the deal on no "Mini-Me No. 3." The mastermind behind my vasectomy.

And let me tell you, it was quite the experience. Lying there on the table, feeling a bit like a prized bull at a livestock auction, knowing that this was it— the end of my super-sperm's reign of terror. There's something oddly humbling about having your bits and pieces so clinically examined and then, well, partially decommissioned.

Doc was a pro, though. He was also surprisingly funny. This doc, man, he was as good with a scalpel as a stand-up comedian with a mic.

Picture this: You're in a chilly room, your crown jewels on full display (or as "full" as they can be under the circumstances), and there's a dude ready to play a game of "catch and release" with your balls. You'd think it'd be as tense as a high-stakes poker game, but Doc defused the whole thing with his wisecracks. I swear, he could've had a second career in comedy.

His humor was sharper than the laser he was about to use (yes, I got the new way of doing the thing with lasers instead of scalpel). Like, here I am, every guy's nightmare scenario, and he's cracking jokes like we're old buddies at a bar. It reminded me of this one time in Minnesota, back in 2012. I met this Irish guy, drunk as a lord, who was dishing out life advice like he was the Dalai Lama of the bar scene. He told me, with a straight face and a twinkle in his eye, how he'd drop a third of a Cialis into his morning coffee every single morning. "Just to always be ready," he said.

That guy was a character, a national treasure for the boring place Minnesota is, but Doc? He was in a league of his own.

So, there I was, getting the old snip-snip, chuckling like a madman. And you know what? It made the whole experience bearable, even memorable. I recommended the dude to all my homies—he deserved it.

Through it all, I couldn't help but think about the irony of it. Here I was, a guy who's lived a life full of wild escapades, crazy parties, and close encounters of the feminine kind, now entrusting his lineage to the careful hands of a guy he'll only ever know as "the pain-free laser vasectomy dude."

In a way, it was poetic. The final act in the saga of my rampaging libido.

The doctor was like a concerned bartender, double-checking if I really wanted that last shot of absinthe ordered at 2:28 a.m. "You sure about this, champ? You're only twenty-eight, and people flip-flop more than Joe Biden in election season." But I knew it was the right thing to do. Anyways, I've got a trump card up my sleeve.

Hidden away in a fertility lab in Montreal, there are five frozen embryos, little potential mini-mes, chilling out. Yep, ready for deployment should I decide the world needs another version of me.

Just last week, my wife got an email from the embryo vault—it's like getting a bill for your Buzzfit membership you forgot you had. There it was, a friendly reminder to renew our annual membership to keep these tiny ice cubes on ice. The alternative? Sign off on a form basically saying, "Hey, med students, need something to slice and dice? Have at it."

It's a bizarre feeling, knowing part of you is just hanging out in deep freeze, waiting for a decision. It's like having a backup plan for your genetics. And every year, we get this reminder, like a Netflix nudge: "Hey, you still watching?" Except it's more like, "Hey, you still planning on potentially unleashing more of your DNA into the world?"

The thought of some Red Bull-guzzling, acne-riddled med student, jacked up on enough Adderall to kill a horse, dissecting my potential kid under a microscope is, well, it's something else. It's like a weird sci-fi movie plot, but it's a life. The life of a potential child that could do great things for the world.

So there I was, chief chef of my kitchen kingdom, hacking away at onions like I was auditioning for the next season of *MasterChef Mexico*, when Victoria hit me with a question that nearly made me slice off a finger. "So, babe, should we have just one last?" she said, all casual, smiling, like she was asking if I was going to add parmesan on the pasta.

Me? Well, it's easy. I switched into my award-worthy performance of "Clueless Oli." I've got this act down to a fucking art form. If there was an Oscar for "Best Performance by a Dumbass in a Domestic Setting," I'd be clearing shelf space for my golden statue. Living in a country where the cops are more interested in shaking you down for soda money than upholding the law, I've become a master of playing the confused gringo. My Spanish is plenty good enough for a chat, sure, but acting like I don't understand a word they're saying, I've realized, is the way to go.

When the local cops try their luck with me, hoping to snag a few pesos for their fifth two-liter

Coca-Cola of the day, I crank up the "dumb tourist" act. A few minutes of my best "No comprendo" routine, and they're more frustrated than a cat trying to catch a laser pointer. They usually give up, muttering some racist shit under their breath, off to find an easier target. A better fish to catch.

Back in the kitchen, Victoria was giving me that look, the one that said she was onto my act but wasn't sure whether to laugh or throw a tomato at me. I kept up the charade, knowing that humor usually helps the transition to another subject, shrugging like I was trying to solve a Rubik's cube blindfolded. "One last what, babe? Meatball? Garlic bread? Help me out here."

But deep down, I knew exactly what she was talking about. One last kid. One last roll of the dice. One last shot at adding another mini chaos-causer to our already lively circus. And maybe this time, it would be a little princess, a mini-her.

Automatically, though, my brain went full-blown Matrix mode, crunching numbers and figuring out the financial gymnastics of bringing another milk-guzzling, boob-sucking, diaper-filling tiny human into our already bustling immigrant circus.

It's messed up, right? Since when did the dream of expanding the family become an Excel spreadsheet exercise? It's like the universe is forcing me to play a twisted game of "The Price is Right" with my future kid's upbringing.

And let's face it, the thought of another mouth to feed was enough to make my wallet break out in a cold sweat. In an ideal world, the decision to have a kid would be all about love, not loot. But there we are, in a reality where checking your bank balance is part of the baby-making process. How screwed up is that?

Now, don't get me wrong. If I were swimming in cash like Jeff fucking Bezos, would I be more inclined to have a whole soccer team of tanned, white-skinned babies? Probably. But it's not about being stingy or not wanting to sacrifice my gaming fund for a new Xbox. No, it's deeper than that. It's about the very basic way of living we now have and I don't want to lose.

I'm talking about being able to provide the good stuff—not just any food, but that top-shelf, organic, kissed-by-angels, locally sourced kind of grub. Clothes that haven't been bathed in chemicals.

Shampoo that doesn't double as a toxic waste dump for your scalp. I want the best for my family, not just the basics. Because in 2024, the basics are toxic. And let's be real—quality comes with a price tag. And there's no sign of this price tag ever going down.

As the seconds ticked by, Victoria's eyebrows started doing that thing where they inch higher, like two caterpillars trying to escape her forehead. She was giving me the look that said, "Are you going to answer, or are you too scared to fucking answer me now?" But me? I was still deep in my act, the king of playing dumb, waiting for the other shoe to drop.

Meanwhile, my mind was racing like a squirrel on double espresso. What if this whole thing was a test, a curveball question to see how I'd react? Maybe she was just pulling my leg, ready to burst out laughing and say, "Babe, you know I'm fucking with you, lol."

Feeling the heat, the pressure cooker of Victoria's question turned my brain into mush. I cracked, like an egg in a frying pan, and I blurted out the dream scenario. The only answer that made sense to me. "Listen, babe, if I had my own rancho in Mexico— bunch of cows mooing, goats goating around, chickens doing whatever chickens do, dogs barking, horses neighing, and a badass red pickup truck with white stripes on the side big enough to fill the whole neighbor in the box to top it all off—then yeah, I could see us having a third kid. Heck, I'd even secretly hope for a baby girl. But if it's a boy, well, I guess he'd be my third right-hand man on our little family farm."

I could see Victoria processing it all, her eyes doing that thing where they looked like they were downloading new information.

I know Victoria well enough to predict her next move. She was probably going to make a beeline for the bathroom under the guise of a giant shit that needed to come out asap, but in reality, she was going to be scouring the internet for ranches for sale across Mexico. And you know what? I'm okay with that. My answer wasn't some throwaway line. It was the truth, straight from the heart. There's a lot of things I do in life that aren't okay, but lying to my wife isn't one of them.

I'm sick and tired of the stereotype that dads are always dragging their feet about having another kid, while moms are practically throwing themselves at us for our "precious seed," like we're some kind of fertility gods that they need to keep pleasuring in hopes for a reward. I bet there are plenty of dads out there who'd love to expand their family, but it's not that simple. We've all got our checklist, our conditions for feeling comfortable with bringing another life into this world. We don't want to add to the struggle—you know, the dad pressure—and end up spending even less time with our kids and drifting further from being the "dadass" we aspire to be, all because we didn't think it through.

With each sprog you pop out, though, it's like leveling up in some real-life version of "Fatherhood: The Dadass Game." By the time I got to my second kid, I was like a freaking parenting ninja on many fucking aspects. The first one? Man, that was like stumbling through a minefield blindfolded. I was clueless and immature as you have read throughout my many stories of my dadass life in early stages. I've laid out all the gritty, pants-shitting terror of being a fresh dad in this book, but let me tell ya, the sequel with kid number two was like switching from a horror movie to a Sunday afternoon sitcom. You're still dealing with a tiny human who thinks 3 a.m. is party time and believes their butt is a never-ending poop fountain, but now you're armed with experience. And a bit of a swagger. I built myself a fucking tool chest with breathwork, meditation, and healthier living habits that make me prepared for any shitty scenario a baby can bring.

There's a whole grocery store list of reasons why you should consider having more than one little monster. Let's be real here. I've met a bunch of "only children" in my time, and nearly every single one of them has had a moment where they're like, "Man, I wish I had a brother or sister growing up." And damn right, I fucking get it. Growing up as the lone wolf in the family has got to be lonelier than a one-legged duck in a two-legged duck race.

Unless you're some self-obsessed, navel-gazing sociopath who's all about me, myself, and I, you've got to feel for these solo kids.

All right, time to spit some cold, hard facts here. Surveys have shown that a whopping 65 percent or more of only children wish they had siblings. No shocker there, considering other studies are screaming from the rooftops that having brothers or sisters is like winning the mental health lottery.

We're talking about having a built-in support system, someone to ride the highs and weather the lows with you. Those who grow up with siblings tend to have better mental health, stronger social skills, and overall, they're just more equipped to tackle life. That's not me saying it; it's science.

Take Mary Bell, for example—poster child for the "only child" club and a case study in "What the hell went wrong?" She was flying solo in the sibling department, and look how that turned out. Not exactly a heartwarming tale of childhood bliss.

Growing up as the middle kid, wedged between an overachieving older sister and a hell-raising younger brother, gave me a front-row seat to the parenting roller coaster. My sister, the guinea pig of the family, got the full brunt of our parents' anxiety-ridden, clueless newbie parenting skills. You know the drill—first-time parents, wide-eyed, winging it, and wondering what the hell they've gotten themselves into.

She was a city kid, born in the concrete jungle where life's a never-ending buzz, a blur of noise and cramped living spaces. Then there's me and my bro, hatching out in some sleepy village, where the most action you'd see is a cow wandering off course.

I think it played in the huge difference of personality between my big sister and me. My sister? She's this anxious, control-freak redhead, and before you jump on the "that's just dumb stereotypes" bandwagon and decide to cancel me online, hold your horses, bro. There's some legit science behind this. Hit up the National Library of Medicine; they've got studies showing a link between those crimson locks and the wiring upstairs. It's not just old wives' tales—there's research backing this up.

So, between being the experiment child for our rookie parents, growing up in a sensory overload city, and rocking that redhead gene, my sister was destined to be a different breed. She's about as similar to me as a cactus is to a bouquet of roses.

You want to know a freaky factoid about my sister and me? The only thing my sister and I have in common, other than taking the grand exit from the same maternal escape hatch, is our birth dates. We all decided to crash the party on the 23rd of a month. Yeah, you heard that right. And you know what's even weirder? My brother as well. All three of us, born on the 23rd. What are the odds, right?

But I have a fucking theory about this, and it's where things get a bit eyebrow-raising. This "bizarre" coincidence means one very interesting thing: my parents must have had a pretty damn consistent schedule when it came to getting frisky in the sheets. I'm talking about precision, like they had a calendar with Xs and Os marked on it—Xs for the days to go all in but pull out, Os for the days to steer clear or stick to oral stuff, and one big, bold cross on that magical day guaranteed to result in a mini-me popping out nine months later, right on the 23rd. In other words, creampie day.

I mean, there's got to be some serious planning behind this. We're not talking about random luck here; this is strategic baby-making. It's like they had the whole thing down to a science—a baby-making algorithm that churned out 23rd-born kids.

So, every time our birthday rolls around, it's not just a celebration of us getting older; it's like a weird tribute to my parents' oddly precise sex schedule. It's one of those family quirks that you don't really want to think too hard about, but once you do, it's like, "Damn, Mom and Dad are fucking weirdos."

Other than this fucked up fact, my relationship with my sister is... Let's just say it's about as warm as a handshake with a snowman. We barely talk, and honestly, it's a bit of a bummer. But it is what it is. The only time we manage to be in the same room without setting off World War III is at those family shindigs—the ones I hardly ever make it to now that I'm living the expat life.

But when I do show up, it's like my parents have come up with this unspoken strategy. They know the only way to keep the peace between me and sis is either to stuff our faces with food so we're too busy chewing to talk or get us locked into a family board game that's as politically neutral as Switzerland. Because, let me tell you, our chats? They're like trying to mix oil and water—it just doesn't work.

She's so far left on the political spectrum, I'm half expecting her to show up one day with blue hair, a septum piercing, and a tote bag full of vegan animal rights propaganda. Meanwhile, I'm parked on the complete opposite end of that spectrum. We're talking polar opposites here.

Core values? Forget about it. While I'm doing everything in my power to keep my kids away from the clutches of the system, she's right there in the thick of it, shaping young minds as a schoolteacher in that very system I've been bashing my whole fucking life. And Big Pharma? Don't get me started. She's got more prescriptions to her name than I've got ink on my skin. It's like she's a walking advertisement for everything I'm trying to steer clear of. I have as much trust in modern-day doctors with their prescription pads than she has trust in me for filing my taxes properly for the government to get all the money I'm supposed to hand out to them.

Growing up, it was the same story. Her sappy romance movies? Made me want to gag. Her shitty commercial Franco pop music playlist? A fast track to a headache. And her friends? Let's just say none of them made my heart skip a beat, all 4/10. Zero incentive to hang out in her orbit.

But that's how it goes, right? More often than not, if you've got more than one sibling, you're gonna vibe with one more than the other. For me, it's my younger brother—he's been my right-hand man since day one. He's my partner in crime, the Robin to my Batman. With him, it's always been easy, like we're on the same wavelength. With my sister? Might as well be broadcasting on different planets.

So if I had to only base sibling relationships on my sister and me, I wouldn't be advocating for big families with multiple little mini-mes. But the relationship between my brother and me is what keeps tiring me in the direction of having more kids.

My little bro, he's three years younger than me, but guess what? The dude's as bald as a cue ball. His nickname might as well be Mr. Clean. Seriously, he drew the short straw in the hair department. Started losing his locks before he even hit the big two-oh. Talk about a raw deal. Poor guy. But hey, the universe decided to split the good genes between him and me. While I got blessed with a decent head of hair, still rocking the long full set of hair at thirty, he ended up with the height. I'm down here rocking the short king life, can't dunk to save my life, and there he is, a towering six-foot-two—not so tall that he's a walking skyscraper freak, but enough to make a room take notice.

We've always been tight, him and me. I can't dig up too many childhood memories—thanks to years of my favorite cocktail of weed, booze, and the good ol' cocaine wreaking havoc on my brain cells—but I remember we were as thick as thieves, always messing around with whatever toys we could get our hands on. And we were into the same shit too. Legos, army guys, cars, dinosaurs—you name it, we were all over it, real alpha male stuff.

Then came the teenage years, and man, did we turn everything into a fight. Every game we played morphed into some kind of bootleg WWE showdown. Soccer matches ended with the wrong set of balls getting a punt, tennis turned into a racquet-smashing melee, and don't even get me started on *Goldeneye* sessions on the N64—those controllers saw more action as weapons than as gaming tools. But despite all the testosterone-fueled chaos, we kept coming back for more. There was something about that rough-and-tumble brotherly love that just worked for us.

Looking back, I can't help but think I wasn't always the best role model for the kid. At least until I got my shit together. For example, if I hadn't been so intense about tattoos, turning myself into a walking ink canvas before I could legally drink and open my fist barbershop inside a tattoo shop, he probably would've waited a bit longer before getting inked himself. Instead, the guy's practically sprinting to the tattoo parlor the minute he turns eighteen. Sorry, Mom.

And let's talk about the music. I'm the one who introduced him to the soul-crushing, world-hating anthems of heavy metal with singers yelling lyrics about life sucking balls and the planet needing a fresh plague—not the most uplifting influence. Maybe, just maybe, he would've been a bit less of a grumpy teen if his big bro wasn't blasting tracks about existential despair at max volume all the freaking time.

The bald giant, he still ended up turning out pretty damn awesome, if I do say so myself. And it's not just because he's been following in my legendary footsteps. The guy's been up to some rad stuff lately, and it's got me beaming with pride like a stage mom at a beauty pageant.

He's shacked up with a girl he's totally smitten with—like, seriously, they're so cute together it's borderline nauseating. He's out there hugging trees, getting all chummy with Mother Nature, finally fucking connecting to real stuff, trotting around the globe like he's on some kind of endless summer vacation, drinking wine in Italy and sipping tequila in Guatemala. Ditched his soul-sucking gig at a mainstream news joint to work for an NHL team— talk about trading up.

But let's get one thing straight that needs to change: The dude still eats like a teenager with his first paycheck. I'm talking a diet that's a heart attack waiting to happen with more microwavable food than any human should consume. And does he listen to any of my health tips? Hell no. Thinks I'm preaching some hippie-dippie nonsense. I guess he has something against living forever. But hey, he's young, he's got time to figure out veggies aren't the enemy.

Now, I'd love to take a bow and claim all the credit for how he turned out, because let's face it—he wasn't exactly taking notes from our parents or my older sister. Why would he? He's about as similar to them as a cactus is to a bouquet of roses. Nah, he's got that same "bum" vibe I've been rocking for years. We're more alike, him and me, than any other family members. But, in all seriousness, I like to think I've been a decent role model later on in life, especially after I got my act together—started a business, got married to my gorgeous wife, popped out a couple of awesome kids, and did all that inner shadow work that make me a badass human.

Even though we're now living in different countries, we're tight. We drop "I love yous" like we're in some sappy rom-com, and there's this unspoken bro-code that we've got each other's backs, no matter what. That's the real deal of brotherhood—it's not about who's got the better hairline (I do) or who can dunk a basketball (spoiler: neither of us; he needs more veggies).

And watching my own boys, Landon and Skyler, I see a lot of that same brotherly chaos brewing. They're like two peas in a pod, if those peas were constantly wrestling and arguing over who's turn it is to choose the songs to play in the car. Gives me déjà vu, and not gonna lie, it's pretty entertaining to watch. I see them, and I think, "Yeah, they're gonna be all right."

My wife and I, we've already cooked up two little hell-raisers who are hella closed knit, right? They're like a miniature Dumb and Dumber, minus the low IQ. If we've nailed it this far, whipping up a third one to add to the mix should be a walk in the park. I mean, why the hell not? Let's turn this dynamic duo into a trio, create our own little band of merry musketeers.

I'm seriously tossing this idea around in my head.

I've been hammering away at this keyboard, churning out over 50,000 words, trying to sketch out the ultimate blueprint for becoming a real Dadass, true and tested. We're talking about a step-by-step guide that takes you from the "I might want kids someday" phase to the full-blown chaos of raising a pack of wild, yet wonderfully positive, future leaders. This book's got it all: mental strategies, physical tips, spiritual insights—you name it. I don't have all the answers but I have faith that every dad can be fucking amazing.

Every single word, every piece of advice, every dad joke I've stuffed in here, it all boils down to one thing, and it's as simple as it gets: love.

See, you can read all the parenting books in the world, go to fucking therapy, quit all the shitty habits in your life, and meditate till you're blue in the face, but if you don't have love at the core of it all, you're just spinning your wheels. Love's the fuel that keeps the Dadass engine running. It's what gets you up at 3 a.m. for diaper duty, what makes you sit through the 100th viewing of *Frozen*, and what has you proudly wearing macaroni necklaces like they're high-end jewelry.

And the best part? It doesn't matter where you're starting from. Even if you feel like a loser dad right now or that you'll be the worst one ever known to humankind. You could be as clueless as a fish out of water when it comes to kids, or you might think you need a major overhaul to even come close to being dad material. But none of that matters if you've got love on your side. It's like the ultimate equalizer, the thing that levels the playing field.

Love's the thing that turns regular dudes into superheroes. For one kid or fifteen...love doesn't get split in multiple kids. It simply multiplies.

You got this, dude. Welcome to the Dadass club.

Love you!

Printed in the USA
CPSIA information can be obtained
at www.ICGtesting.com
LVHW030724080524
779504LV00003B/4